PENGUIN PLAYS

PL41

FAIRY TALES OF NEW YORK

J. P. DONLEAVY

FAIRY TALES OF
NEW YORK

J. P. DONLEAVY

PENGUIN BOOKS

Penguin Books Ltd, Harmondsworth, Middlesex
AUSTRALIA: Penguin Books Pty Ltd, 762 Whitehorse Road,
Mitcham, Victoria.

—

First Published 1961

—

Copyright © J. P. Donleavy, 1961

All performing rights in this play are owned by the author and
permission to give amateur or professional performances must be
obtained from him, c/o Penguin Books Ltd,
Harmondsworth, Middlesex

—

Made and Printed in Great Britain
by Cox & Wyman Ltd
London, Fakenham and Reading

CONTENTS

★

FAIRY TALES OF NEW YORK *was first per-formed at the Pembroke Theatre-in-the-Round, Croydon, 6 December 1960 and transferred to the Comedy Theatre, London, 24 January 1961 with the following cast:*

FIRST ACTOR   BARRY FOSTER

SECOND ACTOR   ROBERT AYRES

THIRD ACTOR   HARRY TOWB

ACTRESS   SUSAN HAMPSHIRE

DIRECTOR: PHILIP WISEMAN

SETTING BY ASSHETON GORTON

★

CONTESTANTS

*

First Actor	CORNELIUS CHRISTIAN	*Act One, Two, Three, Four*
Second Actor	1ST STEVEDORE	*Act One*
	CUSTOMS MAN	*Act One*
	NORMAN VINE	*Act One*
	STEPHEN MOTT	*Act Two*
	ADMIRAL	*Act Three*
	FRITZ	*Act Four*
Third Actor	2ND STEVEDORE	*Act One*
	3RD STEVEDORE	*Act One*
	HOWARD HOW	*Act Two*
	MIKE O'ROURKE	*Act Three*
	CHARLIE	*Act Four*
Actress	ELAINE MUSK	*Act One*
	MISS KELLY	*Act Two*
	GERTRUDE GENTLE	*Act Three*
	CHARLOTTE GRAVES	*Act Four*

ACT ONE

Helen

*

Scene One: THE PIER

Three o'clock, cold February afternoon, a pier, West 27th Street, New York City. Blasts of ships' whistles in the North River. Grinding winches, chatter of greeting people. Rumble of luggage-laden handcarts, and a clinking of chairs. Next to two bags CORNELIUS CHRISTIAN *stands apostate under the letter C.*

1ST STEVEDORE [*voices from behind mountainous crates*]: Hey, Marty, what's in this box, somebody dead? Maybe we ought to be respectful and take off our hats.

2ND STEVEDORE: Don't be crazy, nobody's dead.

1ST STEVEDORE: Yeah? Feel the weight of it. Hey, I heard about this. See that guy over there watching? That's the husband. Wife's in here.

2ND STEVEDORE: Honest?

1ST STEVEDORE: Yeah, honest.

2ND STEVEDORE: Holy mackerel.

1ST STEVEDORE: So move that trolley. Easy. Boy you— need glasses. This is a guy's wife, don't drop it.

2ND STEVEDORE: I should live so long.

1ST STEVEDORE: Shut up, maybe you won't. There what did I tell you. Over there see, customs is going over to him.

LOUDSPEAKER: Now hear this. All passengers are asked to remain under their letters until customs has examined their baggage, please. This will help clear pier. Thank you.

CUSTOMS MAN [*crossing to Christian, a gentle touch on the shoulder*]: I'm sorry, sir, about this. I know it isn't a time you want to be annoyed by a lot of questions, but if you could just give me some information I'll try to get this over as quickly as possible. It's just a formality. [*Raising clip board, writing*] I understand this happened aboard ship?

CHRISTIAN: Yes.

CUSTOMS MAN: And your wife was English and you're an American?

CHRISTIAN: Yes.

CUSTOMS MAN: And you intend burial here?

CHRISTIAN: Yes.

CUSTOMS MAN: It's just that we've got to make sure of these things because it can save a lot of trouble later on. Don't want to burden you with anything unnecessary. Do you have any children travelling?

CHRISTIAN: Just my wife and myself.

CUSTOMS MAN: I understand. And are all your other possessions your own property, all personal effects. No fine art, antiques. You're not importing anything?

CHRISTIAN: No.

CUSTOMS MAN: Just sign here. Won't be anything else and if you have any trouble at all don't hesitate to get in touch with me right away. [*Taking out a card*] Here's my name and I'll straighten out any difficulty. Just Steve Kelly, customs'll get me. Vine Funeral Home phoned here just a while ago. I told him everything was all right and they say you can go see them at their office or phone any time this afternoon or tonight.

CHRISTIAN: Thanks very much.

CUSTOMS MAN: Have you got a porter?

CHRISTIAN: No.

CUSTOMS MAN: Look. See the stevedore there. Guy with fur jacket. I'll send him over. He'll take care of you. O.K. Don't worry about anything. [*A hand on Christian's shoulder.*]

CHRISTIAN: Thanks.

3RD STEVEDORE [*walking up to Christian*]: Excuse me. Steve Kelly, the customs guy. You want some help? This your's here?

LOUDSPEAKER: Now hear this. Please load away from entrance. Please keep the entrance clear for passengers. Please.

CHRISTIAN: Yes. This is mine.

3RD STEVEDORE: O.K. You in a hurry?

CHRISTIAN: No.

3RD STEVEDORE: O.K. You don't mind if we wait a few minutes. Until some of these eager beavers get off this pier. Then you won't have to get crushed and get your bags broken in the rush. They come off this ship like a bunch of starving animals.

CHRISTIAN [*taking out wallet, tendering a dollar*]: Here.

3RD STEVEDORE: I don't want any money. This is strictly a favour. I don't take money for a favour. You'll do the same for somebody. That way it goes round the world.

CHRISTIAN: Thanks.

3RD STEVEDORE: Forget it. Where do you have to go?

CHRISTIAN: I don't know. Have to think of somewhere.

3RD STEVEDORE: A million hotels.

CHRISTIAN: I think I better look for a boarding-house.

3RD STEVEDORE: A boarding-house for a guy like you? You don't look the kind of guy stays in a boarding-house, don't sound it either. You come all the way here without having a place to go? None of my business. O.K. Maybe you got no friends. Takes all sorts of people to make a world. Keep telling my wife that, she don't believe me. Thinks everybody's like her. Across there long?

CHRISTIAN: Went to college.

3RD STEVEDORE: Good education over there. Don't you feel lonely?

CHRISTIAN: No, don't mind being alone.

3RD STEVEDORE: That right. Guy's got a right to feel that way if he wants. Free country. But hear the noise out there [*traffic, hawkers*]. It's going to explode any minute. Place full of dangerous maniacs. [*Looks around.*] You know on this pier. Boy, if you even sneeze at the wrong time. What a life. You keep going, keep going. Like clock springs. They just wind you right up. I used to have a pet shop. I love animals. Yeah. Tell a relative about it. Gets big ideas how to make a lot of money. And I lose the whole thing. And I'm on the pier pushing a cart where every guy's after a fast buck and they kick in your teeth and pull them out of your mouth and your life aint worth a dime. [*A stevedore passing with a handcart.*] Hey, Charlie, can I borrow that a second.

CHARLIE: Drop dead.

3RD STEVEDORE [*to Christian*]: See. Friendship. Means a

lot around here. [*Looks at tag on Christian's bag.*] That's a funny name, Christian. You got a bit of a funny voice too, you English. Learn to speak at college.

CHRISTIAN: Just a bit.

3RD STEVEDORE: That ain't the accent you were born with. Sounds O.K. anyway. People born speaking like that?

CHRISTIAN: I don't know.

3RD STEVEDORE: Maybe I'm asking personal questions. But you're the kind of guy I would have been proud to walk into my pet shop. Those animals I really loved them. They have personalities. All the little funny things they do. [*Distant siren*] Hear that? Guy just murdered his mother for a dollar. And I got to drink milk all day, live like a baby. Just because I don't want to hurt people. Is that bad that I don't want to hurt people. And that I love animals. Now my wife's relatives want me to go into air conditioning. Be a millionaire. Just like with the pet shop. They said all you have to do is feed these dumb animals – get them a big farm. And they get babies like mad. I get the farm for the animals to have the babies. They smell my relatives around the place and they don't want to have any babies. How do you like that? And I go broke. Hey, what am I doing telling you my life's history? You're young, you got life ahead of you. [*Looks that long at Christian, and in the sudden silence looks around.*] Hey, pier's clear. Let's go. [*Picks up bags. Exit.*]

CURTAIN

CORNELIUS CHRISTIAN *sitting, waiting. Hands folded, head gently bent. Coat collar up.*

CHRISTIAN: Come all the way to a funeral parlour, after all these years. So tired. All I've got left of Helen are just her bag of clothes. I mustn't cry. No one to be with her. And I was so full of dying myself. How much is it going to cost? Only thing to do is wait, wait, wait. Helen could never pack things. I told her she was sloppy, why don't you fold things up? [*Takes out wallet.*] What's his name? Norman Vine, funeral director. What do I say to him? Do I have to give him a tip or cigar? Might think I'm not sorry enough and can't concentrate on the death. [*Roar of elevated train*] I could have stepped right under a train. Just let it roar right over me. I'd be electro- cuted. How would they know to take me here and put me with Helen. Ought to write it in my wallet. In case of death take me to Vine Funeral Home and bury me with Helen. So slaughtered you could put me round her in the same casket. [*Hand to brow and eyes.*] I just can't bear for you to be cold and you said last thing of all to put you in the ground. Always wore a green shadow around your eyes. And when you came near me in your silk rustling dress you sounded hollow inside. Shout at you and my voice would come back in echoes. The first day at sea, listening with her eyes, and I didn't want to spend the two dollars for a deck-chair. And I'd let her have it. I'd let her have anything now. Helen, you could have got two deck-chairs or three and I'd have said nothing because I wouldn't be so lonely for you now.

It wasn't the money. I just didn't want you to get cold because you looked so ill you'd freeze up there and no one knew how sick you were. We fought over a towel. I pulled it right out of your hands when you said you'd spend the two dollars. It wasn't the money, I'd tear up two dollars right here in this room. [*Christian's head slumps forward, raises slowly.*] God it was the money. I've lost you. Two rotten bucks.

VINE [*entering room*]: Good evening, I'm Mr Vine. Sorry to keep you waiting. You're Mr Christian aren't you? [*Offering hand.*]

CHRISTIAN [*slowly raising head*]: Yes.

VINE: Are you all right?

CHRISTIAN: Yes. I'm all right. Dusty city. Guess it's blown in my eyes.

VINE: Make yourself comfortable.

CHRISTIAN: Thanks.

VINE: There are only a few little things here, a couple of documents. Customs man who dealt with you telephoned after you left the pier. Very nice of him, and I'll certainly do everything I can Mr Christian. [*Offering papers*] Only these to sign.

CHRISTIAN: Thanks. [*Looks down, through and away from forms.*]

VINE [*gently holds pen out to Christian*]: Here.

CHRISTIAN [*coming back from miles away*]: Thanks.

VINE: I'm not just an ordinary man in this business. It means a great deal to me and if there is any special help I can give anyone I'm really glad to do it. So understand that. If there's anything you want to tell me. Just talk. That helps.

CHRISTIAN: That's nice of you.

VINE: We can only do our best, Mr Christian. Just the best. We understand sorrow. I've arranged burial at Greenlawn. Do you know New York?

CHRISTIAN: Yes, I was born here.

VINE: Then you may not be without knowledge of Greenlawn. One of the most beautiful cemeteries in the world, and it's always a pleasure to visit. Out there where there is much grass and trees the grind of the city is left behind. My wife's buried there as well and I know it's a place of great peace. We realize sorrow, Mr Christian. I'll take care of all the immediate details for you and you can have a chat with them later on. All under my personal direction. Arranged as soon as you wish.

CHRISTIAN: Could it be arranged for tomorrow morning?

VINE: Yes. Will it give mourners time? The notice will only be in tomorrow's *Daily News*, only give anybody couple hours to get here.

CHRISTIAN: I'll be the only mourner.

VINE: I see.

CHRISTIAN: No one knew we were coming to New York.

VINE: We'll use this [*hand out*], the Emerald suite.

CHRISTIAN: I want to keep it very short.

VINE: I understand. In the way of flowers?

CHRISTIAN: I'd like something simple. Perhaps a wreath with 'My Helen'.

VINE: Of course. Something simple. I'll see to it myself. We try to make friends with sorrow, Mr Christian. That way we come to know it. You'd like us to use glass. For permanence.

CHRISTIAN: That's all right.

VINE: And where are you located?

CHRISTIAN: Near the Museum of Natural History.

VINE: I'm pleased you're near there. There's much to reflect upon in that building. We'll send our car for you.

CHRISTIAN: Is that anything extra?

VINE: Included, Mr Christian. Shall I make it nine-thirty, Ten? Whenever you wish.

CHRISTIAN: Nine-thirty is fine.

VINE: Mr Christian, would you like now to have a little drink before you go? Some Scotch or Irish?

CHRISTIAN: Well, thank you, I would. Are you Irish, Mr Vine?

VINE [*crossing to a cabinet*]: My mother was. My father's German. [*Returning with glasses*] Soda?

CHRISTIAN: Please.

VINE: Now the way you said that. Just one word. I can tell by your voice that you're an educated man Mr Christian. I also like your name. I never had very much in the way of education. I was a wildcatter in Texas and then became manager of an oil field. Wouldn't think it to look at me would you? I left school when I was nine years old. And I've always wanted to be in this business. But I was thirty before I got a chance to do a high school course. Did it in the navy and then I went to morticians school when I came out. It makes you feel closer to people. It's dignified. And art. When you see what you can do for someone who comes to you helpless. And to recreate them just as they were in life. Makes you able to soften things. You're a man I can talk to. You're a person who's got a proper mental attitude. I can always tell. There are some of them who make you sick. It's

the only thing I don't like about the business are the
phonies and I get my share of them. Here [*offering drink*],
have another do you good. [*A sparkling tinkling replenish-
ment.*]

CHRISTIAN: Thanks.

VINE: Some people think I'm outspoken but I've given a
lot of satisfaction and people put their whole families in
my hands, even in a big city like this. I opened up
another branch in the West Fifties. But I like it best
here where I began. My two little girls are growing
up into big women now. You meet people from all
walks of life. I'm a bit of a philosopher and I feel anything you've got to learn you'll learn just through what
you have to do with people, in that way I never miss an
education. It's a fact, I never graduated. It's especially
sad when I bury those who did. But everything is how
a person conducts themselves. That's how I know all
about you, customs man said over the phone you were
a real gentleman. Would you like now for me to tell
you something about the establishment? If you don't
it's all right.

CHRISTIAN: I don't mind.

VINE: You'd like to feel that she was somewhere where
she's really at home. We're empty now, there's just two
reposings on at my other branch although it's a busy
time of the year. [*Rising, expanding*] I never want to
have an establishment of mine get so big you lose the
personal touch. It must be warm and intimate to make
people feel at home. I call the other branch a home, bit
of an expense to change here because parlour is in the
neon sign. I feel parlour is a word that lets you down.

18

Something poor people have. I like the word home. I don't gloom at people, I smile. Death is a reunion. A pause in the life of others. You understand me?

CHRISTIAN: Yes.

VINE: This suite here has its own private rest room. Which has been of great success. I wouldn't say it to most people but certain functions get stimulated at the passing of a cherished one. You've noticed how I've used green light and how it glows from the walls, it's a special kind of light that makes it do that. Only kind in New York. You don't mind me talking.

CHRISTIAN: No, it's all right.

VINE: In a few years I'm opening a branch out in the country. For some people the country signifies peace. You perhaps saw that picture out in the hall. The Forest in the Winter Sun. Looking at that in my spare time gave me the idea. It's not conducive to peace to come in off the street to mourn. [*Roar of train*] You hear that elevated train out there? Thinking of tearing it down. Won't be too soon for me. Shakes the teeth out of your head. But I learned to accept it. And also I hope to have a chapel here. And it will be round just like the world and again green will be my motif. I would like the whole establishment to have the air of a studio.

CHRISTIAN: It's all very nice.

VINE: That makes me feel good. I'm pleased. And I hope you'll be satisfied you dealt with me. I always want people to feel that. You can trust me and know I've got reverence for my work. To love your work is happiness. It means I meet someone like you too. I'm never wrong about people. I know the real tears of death and they don't go down the cheeks. And [*looking about in senti-ment*] this is the first room I've ever used. One or two personages been here. Mr Selk the manufacturer. I had that privilege. And we light a candle behind that green glass when someone is reposing. I think it gives, or rather, let me say, lends a sacredness to the occasion.

CHRISTIAN: Yes it does.

VINE [*touching Christian's elbow*]: You go home now. Put all bother out of your head. Get a good night's sleep. Remember it takes time. But time is a friend of ours. And I'm here, remember that, for any kind of request. Our car will be there in the morning.

> [*Light fading. Faintly strains of Beethoven's Fifth Piano Concerto, second movement. Handshake. Vine handing a catalogue*]

Take this. Good night, Mr Christian.

CHRISTIAN [*leaving*]: Good night. [*Roaring elevated train*]

> [*Night comes. A long darkness. A light rises, a green fluttering glow around Helen's coffin. The profile of her white face.* ELAINE MUSK *enters, touches coffin, looks at Helen. Bends to the floral decoration, fixes a flower. She turns to a sound, looks at door.* CORNELIUS CHRISTIAN *enters.*]

ELAINE: Mr Christian?

CHRISTIAN: Yes.

ELAINE: I'm Elaine Musk, Mr Vine's assistant. May I take your coat.

CHRISTIAN: I think I'll keep it on. For a moment.

ELAINE: The music hasn't begun yet. But I'll tell Mr Vine you're here.

> [CHRISTIAN *turns to side of room. Takes off gloves.*

MUSK *watching.* CHRISTIAN *turns to her.* MUSK *softly withdraws.* CHRISTIAN *sits at side of room. Elbows slowly on knees. Head lowered and held between hands.*]

CHRISTIAN: Helen, I wouldn't have brought you to a room like this. Makes me feel I'm casting some poverty on her because this isn't the type of place she would ever be. Hers were fields and open meadows. All this shining junk. Like pies, peaches or eggs. Helen's not a pie, peaches or eggs. She's mine. And taking her away. Gone already. Where is she nearest to me. Asleep on top of my brain. Came with me all over the ship when I couldn't stand them staring at me everywhere I went and whispering. Our table out in the centre of the dining-room. They were all thinking of the day when they had the gala occasion with the paper hats and balloons and Helen just sat there at the table and wept, pink handkerchief tucked up your sleeve and pearls like tiny drops from your face and none of them ever saw you again. They even came up to my cabin door after you were dead to listen to hear if I was crying. And the steward who said they wouldn't do your washing. He stuck his brown face in the door and closed it quietly when he saw me prostrate on the bunk. And he slammed the door in your face. Both of us utterly helpless, could do nothing, could say nothing. I held the three dollars in my fist and watched his brown hand come up from his side and pull them out and leave quietly closing the door. The waiter who filled our plates with things we didn't want and came over the second day and said your wife don't eat no more and I said no. And lunch-time he came back saying he was sorry he didn't know, the wine waiter just told him and he got me a plate covered in smoked salmon. He kept as far away as he could until the last meal when hovering for his tip he asked me if I was a refugee. Then I went out, from the ship's rails I looked at the strange flat shore with the fragile white fingers in the sky. In that cabin, Helen, where you left your soul and I've got to sit here helpless with and without you. [*Standing*] Shut that casket. Screw it down.

VINE: Is there something wrong, Mr Christian?

CHRISTIAN [*sitting, shaking head*]: No.

VINE [*during first half-minute, second movement, Beethoven's Fifth Piano Concerto*]: It's my favourite music I've chosen. She's very beautiful. [*Beckons to casket.*] She's waiting for you. [*Offering hand to shake.* CHRISTIAN *shakes.*] And just press the button there when you want me. All right? [VINE *leaves.*]

CHRISTIAN [*looking at his hand*]: Almost broken my knuckles. Gone so dark. That green light flows and flickers all over the room. Even has my flowers lit up. He must rake in the money. I'm glad the casket's black. I'd die if it were green. [*Goes to kneel at casket.*] So soft kneeling here and I can't look at you. See just the tips of your knuckles. You don't have to shake Vine's hand. If you'd move. You can't get up. Forgive me because I haven't got the courage to look at you. Because I'd see you dead for ever. What happens to all the flesh and blood? No child. You leave nothing but the pain of missing you and because I didn't want the expense. A baby costs money. I wouldn't part with a penny. Only reason I had. I knew you were begging me and I'd always say let's wait. And we waited. Your casket's so smooth. Put my hand along the bottom to see if it's stuck with chewing gum. Vine would never allow that. And although he must be half crazy he's given me comfort because I don't feel you're laughed at or joked over dead. Got to keep my head down or I'll look by accident. Thought I would cry and I can't. Helen, I wish we were different from everybody else. Scream for some sort of thing that makes us you and me. Neither of us nothing. And on the ship you said you wanted to lie down in the cabin. Those first Americans you met just tired you out, Helen. And I was so proud of bringing you back to my country. I wanted you to like them. And even after you'd gone, you don't want anyone to come and touch you on the arm and say I'm sorry about it, about your wife, have courage or something, but you do want them. I wanted someone to show me something. Anything. But not a soul on that damn ship came near me except for money. Each second you get farther away from me. And now they dig the hole with the straight sides and before it gets dark you'll be covered up. And all the times I wished you were dead. So I could be free. But those were black thoughts of anger. But I thought them. Must get up. [*Stands, goes to curtain, pulls back from window.*] Busy street. Izzies Best for Bargains. And Vine has a green handkerchief in his pocket. What has he got against the colour green? Most of his life must be whispering, nodding, hand-rubbing, and the five words we'll take care of everything. Except the bill. Think pure. Think straight. Be red-blooded. Big-hearted. Glad-handed. Show them you can take it. And Vine will open up a country place called Green Beacon.

[VINE *entering quietly, slowly to casket. Leans over with handkerchief.*]

VINE: Must be a little condensation on the inside, Mr Christian. But I hate anything to mar such a lovely face. Woman's lips are one of the most beautiful parts of her body. I can always tell a woman who looks at a man's lips when he talks instead of his eyes. Are you all right, Mr Christian?

CHRISTIAN: Yes, I'm all right. Do you think we could leave now?

VINE: Yes, a few minutes. Our large reposing room is busy this morning. We never know in this business.

CHRISTIAN: Mr Vine, I think maybe you're telling me too much about your business. I don't want to say anything, but it's getting me down.

VINE: What's the matter?

CHRISTIAN: I don't want to know about the business. It's getting me down.

VINE: Don't get sore, Mr Christian. I forget sometimes. I try to make everyone feel at home and not treat the funeral business as something strange. People ought to know about it. My own funeral is already arranged. I thought you'd take an interest. But don't get sore. When it happened to me and it was my wife I found I needed some sort of distraction and because I arranged the services myself it made me feel better. I thought you wanted to take an interest.

CHRISTIAN: This isn't distraction.

VINE: Take it easy, son. Easy now. You're not alone in this, remember that. If I shot my mouth off I'm sorry. I don't want to do that with anybody, but getting sore isn't going to bring her back. Beauty is the only thing you can remember. Try to remember beauty. Come on, I like you, be a sport.

CHRISTIAN: My wife's dead.

VINE: I know that.

CHRISTIAN: Well, what the hell do you mean, sport?

VINE: I hope I understand you correctly, Mr Christian, you would now rather I didn't conduct this any further. I can put you in the hands of my assistant, Miss Musk, if you prefer.

CHRISTIAN: All right, all right. I'm not the kind of person who wants to start trouble. Leave everything as it is. I'm just worried about money and what I'm going to do.

VINE: Look. Listen to me. I want to tell you straight. I don't cut cash out of nobody. I don't conduct this business on those lines. You've got as long as you want and longer. Understand me. And if that isn't long enough I'll think of something. If you hadn't come here alone from another country I wouldn't take all this trouble, but you seem to be a nice guy. I even thought you were a type for this profession and that's a compliment as far as I'm concerned. How many of these slobs would think of wearing a green tie like you. You're a gentleman. And when it's over, if you want to come back and see me, I'd like that. There's a place for you here, remember that. And if you make that decision I'd like that. If you want, we'll close it now, Mr Christian. You're ready.

CHRISTIAN: All right.

[VINE *pressing buzzer*, ELAINE MUSK *enters*.]

VINE: We're leaving now, Miss Musk.

MUSK: Very good, Mr Vine.

[MUSK *goes to Christian's coat. Holds it for him to put on.*]

VINE: Mr Christian,

[CHRISTIAN *pulling on his white gloves*]

since you've got no religious preference I might read just a few words of my own at the interment.

CHRISTIAN: All right.

VINE: And I'll be giving a few dollars to the grave diggers if that's all right.

[CHRISTIAN *nods.*]

And perhaps now you will wait with John the chauffeur. We won't be a moment.

[CHRISTIAN *exits.*]

Miss Musk, there's a boy we could use. He's a little upset. Inclined to be nervous. But that's good. He's got the touch. And that's all you need.

CURTAIN

ACT TWO

The Interview

*

Scene One: MOTT'S OFFICE

An April morning. STEPHEN MOTT *leans over and speaks into his desk microphone.*

MOTT: Send in Mr Christian.
  [CORNELIUS CHRISTIAN *collegiately crossing to take Mott's outstretched hand.*]
  Well if it isn't my boy Christian, isn't it?
CHRISTIAN: Yes, Mr Mott, it is.
MOTT: Well, sit down, delighted to see you son. Have a smoke, my boy?
CHRISTIAN: No, thanks.
MOTT: Well, what can I do for you?
CHRISTIAN: Mr Mott I'd like to make money.
MOTT: Ha, ha. Well that's a pretty straightforward, you might say that it's a universal incentive. A word we use a lot around here, I mean incentive. Like that type of word, connotes purpose. Well now. How do you feel we can help? Got something to offer us?
CHRISTIAN: Myself.
MOTT: Well now, another pretty straightforward answer. I like that. It's Cornelius Christian, isn't it.

CHRISTIAN: Yes.

MOTT: Well now, I'll call you Cornelius. Well Cornelius, so you'd like to make money. Come over here.

[CHRISTIAN *to window behind Mott.*]

Down there is the harbour of New York. Just look down there. What put us way up here?

CHRISTIAN: Well I guess the elevator.

MOTT: Boy, I'm talking on a different level.

CHRISTIAN: Oh.

MOTT: Ingenuity. It's a word we use around here. Say it.

CHRISTIAN: Ingenuity.

MOTT: Come on, let's have some lung.

CHRISTIAN: Ingenuity.

MOTT: That's better, boy. I remember you. A party of my son's wasn't it? Couple of months ago. Just back from Europe weren't you? You had a bit of sadness with your wife. Which I was sorry about. I remember that party. The jukebox got short circuited in the rumpus room. Remember a couple comments you made caught my ear? Yeah.

CHRISTIAN: Yes, I was at the party.

MOTT: Look, tell you what. Bit rushed just now, excuse me a second. [*Into desk microphone*] Miss Peep, get me personal, Mr How. [*The large smiles of friendliness in the pause.*] Ah. Hello Howard. Got a young man here, friend of my boy's. He wants to make money. Want you to talk to him and show him around. Thinks we can use him. Yes. Yes. [*Turning to Christian*] Cornelius, you free right now.

CHRISTIAN: Certainly, yes.

MOTT [*into desk microphone*]: All right Howard, you take

care of that. Kids, Howard, O.K.? Fine. Well life will
get less noiser as you get older Howard and the kids
grow up. Great Fine. Great. That's great. O.K. Howard.
Bye. [*Turning to Christian*] Well, Cornelius, our Mr
How will show you around. See what we can do. And
he'll talk it over with you. Maybe we can have a chat
again. I like to talk to the young kids coming along.
Now what's that word.

CHRISTIAN: Ingenuity.

MOTT: 'at a boy, Christian.

CHRISTIAN: Thanks very much, Mr Mott.

MOTT: Any time, Christian.

CHRISTIAN: And hope that spot's a little better.

    [MOTT *surprised*.]

You know the spot you had in front of your eyes, said
you could follow it out the window like it was a bumble
bee only it would always come back again.

MOTT: You got some memory boy.

    [*The long pause that does not refresh*.]

And memory makes money. Remember that utterance.
Words are wonderful. Remember that too.

CHRISTIAN: It's been extremely good of you, Mr Mott.

MOTT: Anything anytime for the young people. Keep in
touch. Find Mr How five floors down.

CHRISTIAN: Thanks again, Mr Mott.

    [MOTT'S *smile*. CHRISTIAN *exits*. MOTT'S *stone face*.]

CURTAIN

HOWARD HOW *studiously at his desk.* CORNELIUS CHRISTIAN *entering.*

HOW: Mr Christian?

CHRISTIAN: Yes.

HOW: I'm Howard How. [*Outstretched hand.*]

CHRISTIAN: Hello. I'm thinking of moving to the Bronx. [CHRISTIAN's *hand goes to lip, my what an utterance.*]

HOW: You're what?

CHRISTIAN: Oh, sorry, Mr How. Guess I'm nervous. I've just strangely had something on my mind about the Bronx. Once it was meadow land, I've been reading an old guide book.

HOW: Oh?

CHRISTIAN: Yes, ha, ha. Was thinking maybe some parts might still be meadow land.

HOW: We manufacture spark plugs, Mr Christian.

CHRISTIAN: Of course, of course. I don't dispute that for a minute.

HOW: And there are no meadows left in the Bronx.

CHRISTIAN: I would never dispute that either.

HOW: What do you dispute?

CHRISTIAN: I don't dispute anything. Nothing at all. Oh, there are some things I don't like, all right. But I don't dispute anything. It was just that when I was looking out of the train [CHRISTIAN *upturns a left supplicant hand*] I just thought once [*looking into hand*] there were real Indians running around here.

HOW: Well let's get back to the twentieth century now.

CHRISTIAN: Sure.

HOW: And you're interested in our using you.

CHRISTIAN: I'd like it if you could.

HOW: Point is, Mr Christian, just what can we use you for. I note you have a rather English tone to your voice. Didn't by any chance pick that up in the Bronx?

CHRISTIAN: As a matter of fact I learned it out of a book.

HOW: Oh. Now look, I'm not trying to hurt your feelings. For what it's worth you might as well know Mr Mott likes to have an English quality about the place. You've noticed the rural scenes of England in the halls. We know how to appreciate that kind of atmosphere here.

CHRISTIAN: Yes, nice and green. I mean, you know, rustic. I like it.

HOW: Glad. We feel it's a nice contrast to the product. Well, aesthetically we've made progress together. Arrived at a nice base to use as a springboard. Now. Well, what, Mr Christian, are you exactly interested in doing. What are your qualifications, your degrees?

CHRISTIAN: Well, as a matter of fact, Mr How.

HOW: Good. The facts. That's what we want, Christian, the facts.

CHRISTIAN [quickly out with the handkerchief to deal with sudden nose tickling]: I just missed, I guess, by only a few subjects of course, getting my degree. At that time I had a lot of things on my mind. You see I've always been deeply interested in human nature and I guess I got distracted.

HOW: Sorry, Mr Christian, but I understand you don't have a degree.

CHRISTIAN: Well. Except of misery I guess. [The leaning forward. The careful agonization.] But I almost made it.

HOW: Don't be alarmed, Christian, these notes I'm making are just a few facts. Note you got alacrity with words.

CHRISTIAN: But I almost made it, I really did.

HOW: Easy, boy. Easy. We make spark plugs. We want to make money.

[CHRISTIAN's *face the setting sun of sincerity*.]

You know, I can see you really do, don't you?

CHRISTIAN: Yes.

HOW: I'm glad your desire is sincere.

CHRISTIAN: Thanks.

HOW: We have progressed. You're a friend of Mr Mott's son, I presume. Mr Mott's a friendly but very busy man and this affair more or less, you understand me, rests in my hands if we're going to find something for you. Do you have any preference as regards production or management?

CHRISTIAN: Well. I'd like to manage, if that can be arranged.

HOW: Just give that pitcher of water a push in my direction will you. Want some water?

CHRISTIAN: Thanks a lot. [*The good things are free*.]

HOW: You got a far-away look in your eye.

CHRISTIAN: Well you see this water's got a history.

HOW: Oh.

CHRISTIAN: You'll think I'm crazy.

HOW: I'm prepared to wait until conclusions are conclusive. Let's hear the water's history.

CHRISTIAN: Well the water has got to come from the Catskills.

HOW: That's fairly common knowledge.

CHRISTIAN: From the Ashokan Reservoir.

HOW: Maybe that fact is not common.

CHRISTIAN: I read in a geography book as a kid what they had to do. Am I boring you?

HOW: Oh, no. I'm fascinated.

CHRISTIAN: Well, I know it's ridiculous but I just can´t forget what it took to make this reservoir. Fifteen thousand acres. Seven villages sunk. Thirty-two cemeteries with two thousand eight hundred bodies they had to dig up.

[HOW *pushing his glass away*.]

And even an eighteen-mile tunnel through the mountains which is one of the longest subterranean aqueducts in the world.

HOW: Boy, you're just full of facts.

CHRISTIAN [*raising glass*]: I guess we might be drinking somebody's soul.

[HOW's *raised head to look towards sunnier thoughts*.]

I'm glad I've had this drink of water. Thanks.

HOW: Don't mention it. [HOW's *licking of the lips*.] We better reconstruct the relationship here. You're still looking for a job.

CHRISTIAN: Oh, yes.

HOW: O.K. We want men with ideas. Ideas more than anything. I may mention along this line that we prefer these ideas to be of a red-blooded nature as opposed to weird. Can you type?

CHRISTIAN: Well. My parents gave me one of those little typewriters when I was a kid but I don't expect that would qualify me as a typist at the moment, but it's something I could pick up. I pick up most things rather easily –

HOW: Like your degree, for instance.

CHRISTIAN: Look, Mr How. I'm after a job. I don't want to misrepresent myself or give a false impression, but as I said I'm interested in human nature.

HOW: You said that.

CHRISTIAN: I don't have a degree. O.K. Maybe I was too distracted by human nature in college. I got disappointed in human nature as well and gave it up because I found it too much like my own.

HOW: Wow, Christian. You're some candidate.

CHRISTIAN: But I wasn't stupid, you know.

HOW: Look, Mr Christian. You don't mind if we don't bother seeing things today. I mean you'll understand that until we know what you can do there isn't really much point in my showing you our set-up at the moment. I know Mr Mott's one of the friendliest men you could ever want to meet and I know he wants to help you, but it is rather a question, in the end, can you help us?

CHRISTIAN: Yes, I understand.

HOW: You're a very presentable person and, of course, well spoken and, by the way, I like the way you tie your knots, that's a nice tie, always be sure of a man in this business if he wears a knitted tie. Just want us both to face the facts. And that suit too. Just the facts, Christian. Just the facts.

CHRISTIAN: O.K.

HOW: Got an opening for a courier representative. [*At papers.*] Dispatch and deliver various important papers. Expenses, taxi, and all the rest.

CHRISTIAN: I'm almost thirty years old. You mean I deliver papers? Like a messenger boy?

HOW: Not in so many words, Mr Christian. Not in so many words. It's of the nature of a confidential dispatch agent and you would, of course, hold the title of executive courier.

CHRISTIAN: What are the friends I've known all my life going to say. They'd be overjoyed. Never stop laughing. I went to college you know.

HOW: A lot, an awful lot of people go to college, Mr Christian. Mr Mott never went to college and he controls a business extending to twenty-nine states – we just added Texas yesterday.

CHRISTIAN: Well, I've had a job before.

HOW: I'm keeping an open mind. I'm perfectly reasonable you know, Mr Christian? What sort of work did you do? You see I'm not here to bring about a stalemate with applicants. I'm here to hire the right man for the right job. O.K.? Now what exactly are you experienced in?

CHRISTIAN: Does it matter?

HOW: That's up to you. I'm only trying to help. Just testing your qualifications. Want to know the sort of work you're best suited for. Where your interests truly lie. We're an outfit you know, where, when it's expedient, we take off our jackets, you understand me, and roll up our sleeves. And being a courier executive would allow your capabilities to rise to the surface. You see what I mean?

CHRISTIAN: To be frank, I've been, well, I'm experienced.

HOW: O.K. But frank with the facts, Christian. How were you used?

CHRISTIAN: They used me, I guess as a sort of

representative, as you might say. A specialist in human relations. As I've said I could count myself as a former student of human nature.

HOW: Yes, I know, you've said that three times now. You were in public relations then.

CHRISTIAN [*an abhorer of relations in public*]: Well yes, sort of, I guess. I wasn't too clear at the time because I had a lot of things on my mind.

HOW: What firm was this?

CHRISTIAN: As a matter of fact –

HOW: That's right, the facts, Christian –

CHRISTIAN: It was called the Stars of the Forest, I guess, Incorporated.

HOW: How's that, boy?

CHRISTIAN: Stars of the Forest.

HOW: Don't mind telling me their product? Briefly.

CHRISTIAN: Death.

HOW: How's that, boy?

CHRISTIAN: Death.

HOW: What?

CHRISTIAN: What I'm telling you, death. One word.

HOW: You mean an undertaker?

CHRISTIAN: Since we're down to one word, yes, an undertaker. A Mr Vine, director of Stars of the Forest, said I excelled in that professional capacity.

HOW: Well you know, God help me, Christian, I honestly don't know what to make of you. Get that chair over there and sit down. It's not been in my experience previous to this to consider anybody in the light, or, forgive me, darkness, of these circumstances. How long did you undertake?

CHRISTIAN: I undertook for, well, not long. I'm begging for a chance to prove myself, Mr How. Just one chance.

HOW: Easy. Take it easy. [*Hand to brow.*] Just got to think. What an interview. I am deeply involved in this disorientation. Just let me ask you a question will you? Wait, excuse me a second. [*Speaking into desk microphone*] Miss Kelly, would you please play over to me the background music we've chosen for Friday's conference for our Chicago representatives.

KELLY [*disembodied*]: Yes, Mr How.

HOW [*Tchaikovsky's Andante Cantabile for strings*]: Cornelius. Now look, tell me, were you looking for this job? Don't have to answer that if you don't want.

CHRISTIAN: Someone close to me died.

HOW: Sorry to hear that. By the way, you like this music?

CHRISTIAN: It's nice.

HOW: Soothes, doesn't it. Guess it's been one of the most successful innovations Mr Mott introduced into business practice, almost like the invention of the wheel.

[*Glum* CHRISTIAN.]

Come on, Cornelius, cheer up. Only thing is we got a problem here. Your job in the funeral parlour business is not going to cut much ice with Mr Mott, in fact the mere mention of it will throw a distinct chill into him. But I'll tell you something before we go any further, you know, I like you, I think you're O.K.

CHRISTIAN: Thanks.

HOW: You know, most of the people sent along to me with pull with Mr Mott aren't worth their weight in paper, strictly between us, you understand. You strike me as a guy with imagination. I'm going to give you a chance.

If I assign you to our idea department, do you suppose you could get some ideas. It'd be a trial, you understand.

CHRISTIAN: Ideas about what?

HOW: Come on, Cornelius, what am I letting myself in for? Quick. Ideas. We make spark plugs. Mr Mott loves the use of words. Think of something. Quick.

CHRISTIAN: My mind's a blank at the moment.

HOW [*into desk microphone*]: Miss Kelly, give us something faster, for a fast idea session of approximately forty-five seconds starting ten seconds from now.

KELLY [*without body*]: Coming ten seconds from now.

CHRISTIAN: Gee, I'm worried. My whole life depends upon what I might say.

HOW: Wouldn't put it like that. Think. One sentence. One idea, a rhyme, anything, don't care what it is, so long as it underlines an inescapable fact.

CHRISTIAN: But all my facts have escaped.

HOW [*Liszt's Hungarian Rhapsody*]: Go, go, boy.

CHRISTIAN: I can't go anywhere, Mr How, I swear it. The facts have escaped.

HOW: Go after them, boy. I know you can do it. Think of something to do with a spark plug. Think of the money. Money, boy. Think of the money.

CHRISTIAN: I am. Wait. If you've got a heart, you've got a spark that could be a heart by Mott.

[HOW *a giant in success*.] [CHRISTIAN, *a sigh, a relaxing back*.]

When you said money, those words just came pouring into my mind.

HOW: Don't be ashamed of that, boy. [*Into microphone*]

Miss Kelly, good, it did the trick, neat selection, make a note of it.

KELLY [*no body*]: Glad it worked, Mr How.

HOW: It was swell. And make a note, we've got a new man for our idea department starting right away.

KELLY [*bodyless*]: Yes, indeed, Mr How.

HOW [*standing, hand extended to Christian, a glad hand. CHRISTIAN's descent into deflation*]: Hey, boy. Hey, there.

CHRISTIAN [*comes to, jumps to take that glad hand*]: Oh!

HOW: You're in. Boy.

CHRISTIAN: Mean I'm hired?

HOW: Of course.

CHRISTIAN: Just like that?

HOW: Just like that.

CHRISTIAN: Well, isn't it too quick? Isn't there something more? Can't I fill something out? I just don't feel it's me.

HOW: Cornelius, I think you've got what it takes. Yes. If you've got a heart, you've got a spark that could be a heart by Mott. Here, gee, have another drink of water. Yes. Ingenuity –

CHRISTIAN [*mouth coming up out of the water which displaced 2,800 dead bods*]: Makes industry.

HOW [*leaning over microphone*]: Miss Kelly, can you hear what's happening in here?

KELLY [*vocal*]: Yes, I can, Mr How. It's wonderful.

HOW: Well, get it down.

KELLY: Got it, Mr How.

HOW: Flash those two things to Mr Mott. He's got to hear about this right away. Ingenuity makes industry. A follow-up to Mr Mott's favourite word.

CHRISTIAN: But this is awful, I mean I feel overrated, just for a few words.

HOW [*looking down an index finger at the level of his eye*]: We find a guy, Cornelius, with words like that coming out of his head, we buy that head.

CHRISTIAN: Mr How, I'm – I think I'd rather be a messenger boy.

HOW [*into desk microphone*]: Miss Kelly, I want you to shout back just what you think of Christian's word formations.

KELLY: They're really impressive.

HOW: Now, boy, hear that?

CHRISTIAN: But I'll tell you the truth –

[HOW *calmly waiting for truth.*]

no, maybe I better not.

[HOW *smiling warmly.*]

But I don't know a thing about spark plugs or industry. Except that there's money in it somewhere.

HOW: Isn't that enough, boy. Money is the moment of truth. Boy. You have saddened my life right now. [*Into desk microphone,* CHRISTIAN *sadder*] Miss Kelly would you make a fresh statement. Just tell him. Exactly what you think.

KELLY [*without body*]: I think he's really spontaneous.

HOW: There you are, boy.

CHRISTIAN: I'm only just a reasonably normal person.

HOW [*the deep concern*]: You're not normal, boy. I know it.

[CHRISTIAN *coming alive.*]

Oh, wait. Hold it. Whoa. Let's reconstruct this relationship here. [*Into desk microphone*] Miss Kelly would you see that Cornelius and myself are left undisturbed here for a few minutes and stop all calls. We just need a little talk.

KELLY [*disembodied*]: Certainly, Mr How, anything for background music?

HOW: Not for the moment thanks. [*To Christian*] Now look, Cornelius, let's sit over here. [*Side by side on leather sofa.*] I'll give it to you straight. When Mr Mott gets these messages he's going to want to see you right away. Now I'm going to risk my life. You know why? Because I like you. When you first came in here I just thought you were another snooty sophisticate out of the ivy leaves. But you know, you've got a real quality in you. Which goes deeper than a shirt and tie.

CHRISTIAN: My job in the funeral parlour, I suppose. But it was the only thing I could get when I first got back from Europe.

HOW: That's what I want to talk about. It's Europe. That's the thing's given you this quality too. A sort of thing that's real. Breeding. But look. I've got absolute faith in you. You could dazzle this industry.

CHRISTIAN: Mr How, thanks, but I think you're making a mistake. I'm not like that at all. That's just the way I appear. Some of the things I really think and believe would revolt you. I'm almost a criminal type.

HOW: What a remark. You're just full of ideas, boy. Why you're not more of a criminal than I am – [CHRISTIAN *alive*] I mean [HOW's *light smile of relief*], I just mean we're alike. But look. I'm maybe ten years older than you. Got wife, kids, nice home out in Long Island. The real things. Sure I've got some gripes. But I'll tell you something. See those binoculars. Want you to look out the window with them. Go ahead.

[CHRISTIAN *to window with binoculars.*]

Towards the Statue of Liberty. Got it? Now a little to the left.

CHRISTIAN: Yes.

HOW: See those barges?

CHRISTIAN: I think so.

HOW: That's refuse. Happens every day, all day. Come down the Hudson and out of East River, filled with stuff that's no more use. They dump it. Christian, it's made an awful impression on me. See, dumped. Maybe not in a river, but you know what I mean.

CHRISTIAN: Mr How I've lost my ambition.

HOW: Boy, don't ever say a thing like that. Not good for you to say it and it's not good for me to hear. Boy and I've heard an earful.

CHRISTIAN: But I mean it, Mr How.

HOW: Call me Howard, Cornelius, as a personal favour I'm asking you right now to take this job. I know everything's going to click. Do it for me. You know, I've got to laugh, here I am begging you to work for us and ten minutes ago I was wondering how I was politely going to discourage you.

CHRISTIAN: Dump.

HOW: Well yeah, but – no, no –

KELLY [*without body*]: Excuse me for interrupting, Mr How, but Mr Mott wants you to come up to his private reception room right away.

HOW: There, boy. [*Into microphone.*] Thanks, Miss Kelly. Right. Now, Cornelius. I'm asking you now, please.

I've got to go through with this now. Just be yourself.
Just let your personality come out as it's done with me.
Only just don't give any hint of your past employment.
Mr Mott's toleration for the suppression of facts is nil,
but to me, it's worth the risk. Just go in with the trace
of a smile, that's all I'm asking you.

[CHRISTIAN's *mumchance mumification*.]

But don't look like that.

CHRISTIAN: I'm O.K., Mr How. [*Softly, Beethoven music.*]
My memory's just working.

[HOW *touched. A long silence.*]

HOW: Yeah. [*Sadness.*] Anyway, just say that thing once
more.

CHRISTIAN: You mean about industry?

HOW: Please. With conviction. Ingenuity makes –

CHRISTIAN: I think I've got something better. Ingenuity
made Mott, Mott makes industry.

HOW: Miss Kelly, get something for my heart, it's missing
beats and get this down, it's Christian again. Ingenuity
made Mott, Mott makes industry.

KELLY [*no body*]: Shall I flash that to Mr Mott?

HOW: No no. He's got a weak heart too.

CURTAIN

Large room. MOTT *sits in low chair. Window behind. Table covered with phones at his elbow. Legs crossed. Holding up his hand for Christian to shake.* CHRISTIAN *walks across and takes it.*

MOTT: Howard, you saw what I didn't see, at first sight that is.

HOW [*slight wringing of the hands*]: It was nothing, Steve. Miss Kelly selected the background music.

MOTT: Sit over there, Christian. [*To a distant seat on Mott's right.*]

[HOW *to a distant seat on Mott's left.*]

Well let's hear all these nice things.

HOW: Steve, he's got something even better, didn't want to flash it.

MOTT: Give us a flash now, Christian.

CHRISTIAN: Ingenuity made Mott, Mott makes industry.

MOTT: Very happy. Very happy indeed. Let's have that once more with lung. Lots of lung.

CHRISTIAN: Ingenuity made Mott, Mott makes industry.

MOTT: Not bad. It's good. Youth refreshes. Of course you don't expect to be paid much for that.

CHRISTIAN: No. But I think it's good.

MOTT: Oh, it's good. Youth refreshes. Well, you're not kidding us, son, I can see that.

HOW: He's not, Steve.

MOTT: No. At the risk of sounding too full of myself, which I do not want to sound. On the other hand I'd like to sketch in my general attitude. Towards the way I personally tackle things. Don't get the idea that I think of myself as a king or anything. But I like to acquire the evidences of man's creative impulse from outside my own orbit. But, sadly, not many are blessed with the creative impulse, but, of course, there's the repulsive creative impulse too. We won't go into that. But if there are bright brains I don't care what kind of head you got the brains in.

[CHRISTIAN *putting a hand to head.*]

Your head's all right, Christian, don't get nervous. But a head, square, ten feet high or like a ping-pong ball is all right so long as it works. But don't let me sound like a king. So I think you have a future, Christian. Now what about the past.

HOW: Steve, I've been through his past with him.

MOTT: Once more, fast, won't hurt.

HOW: Thought we could get around to it later. Past's fine.

MOTT: I'm interested. At that party back there, that night, Christian, you had a lot of pretty pertinent things to say with maybe a few impertinent. What have you been working at?

HOW: Steve.

MOTT: Howard, will you give the boy a chance.

HOW: Steve, do you think, with the pressure of time, that we should discuss this now.

MOTT: It has always been my habit to discuss things now. Because after now might be the hereafter, you get me. Christian's been out of college a while.

HOW: But, Christian, here is a peculiar case.

MOTT: Why?

HOW: I think his creative qualities are rare.

MOTT: That so?

HOW: Well [*a hand towards Christian*], you've heard him yourself, Steve, a natural alacrity with words.

MOTT: Howard, press the button there for the curtains. [HOW *steps to wall, curtain swings open, a pair of binoculars hang.*]

I don't usually show people this. But I want you to look out there, Howard. See any barges out there, going past the Statue of Liberty. Know what they are.

HOW: I think I do, Steve.

MOTT: Well, it's a private little object lesson of mine.

HOW: I understand completely, Steve.

MOTT: Here today, gone tomorrow.

HOW: I completely understand.

MOTT: So now that nobody is misunderstood let's hear about your past career. Not that I'm buying your past, just the future. Nevertheless, past gives indication of future.

CHRISTIAN: Mr Mott, I was employed as the star receptionist for Stars of the Forest Incorporated. A funeral parlour.

MOTT [*turning from Christian to How*]: Howard.

HOW: Yes, Steve?

MOTT: Howard.

HOW: Yes Steve?

MOTT: Howard, I'm talking to you.

HOW: I know, Steve.

MOTT: What about this?

CHRISTIAN: I was expelled from school for lying and cheating. Didn't get my degree from college. And since I've been performing a job in which I conducted the arrangements for those finding their final resting place. And nothing unseemly ever marred proceedings.

HOW: In the nature of human relations, Steve.

MOTT: I've got my own eyes and ears, Howard. There are all kinds of relations. But let me utter three things. Life is for the living. A dime is a dime. And last and the most, a dollar is a dollar. I am not being vulgar mentioning money. I change my shirt three times a day. I also yesterday was on a plane from Washington when the steward asks me was I any relation to the Motts who had a mauseleum at Throggs Neck; when I said yes he tells me his father takes care of it. This is the curiosity of life. But young Christian here tells me he's a liar and a cheat, degreeless, and can smoothly conduct people to their final resting place. Run the Mott empire like a morgue. Now just what exactly do you take me for? Why weren't the facts laid bare in the first instance.

HOW: Don't let facts fool you, Steve.

MOTT: Don't you be too hasty, Howard.

HOW: I feel most recent facts take precedence over previous.

MOTT: I am of the opinion not wanting to be a king about it that past facts forecast future facts.

HOW: You're wrong.

MOTT: Come again, Howard?

HOW: You're not exactly right in judging personalities.

CHRISTIAN [standing up slowly]: I think I'd better go.

MOTT: Stay, Christian. We'll have this out.

CHRISTIAN [standing]: But I didn't think I'd be coming between two people. Breaking up a friendship.

[There are looks between Mott and How. MOTT emits the small chuckle. HOW allows some of his front teeth to show.]

I know this is a business empire, but aren't you two people friends?

MOTT: You have the habit of asking a lot of direct questions.

CHRISTIAN: In the fact-finding maybe I ought to find some, that's all.

MOTT: Those don't sound like the words of a liar and a cheat. I just would like to know what the score is on you, go ahead, sit down. I don't want to be rude or hurt your feelings. But you know underneath this gentle innocent exterior of yours, you seem to throw your weight about. In fact I distinctly feel I'm being pushed. That little remark about friendship and coming between two people. Yeah. And the night at my son's party. You remember my spot. And I remember overhearing a few remarks about my house as well –

[*Oh the look of innocence of* CHRISTIAN.]

don't look innocent, about the new rich vulgarity. And don't think I planned this either, getting you up here with Mr How to give you a working over. I was impressed but don't think that you can push us all over.

CHRISTIAN: What makes you think this –

HOW: Steve, I've never met such a candid fellow as Christian.

MOTT: Oh, you think a fellow is candid because he tells you to your face that he is a liar and a cheat. And sweated away in a funeral parlour guiding people to their final resting places. And with a little background music he starts to spout beautiful utterances. Howard, don't be so naïve. Christian here could dazzle you all night with slogans each one better than the last.

HOW: Wouldn't it be sad then, Steve, to ignore this talent?

MOTT: It just so happens I know Christian's background.

HOW: Steve, please let me in on all of this.

MOTT: You're not surprised, Christian?

HOW: I thought he was an unknown quantity to you, Steve.

CHRISTIAN: Whatever you say, Mr Mott. But I think I really ought to be going.

MOTT: Aren't you going to abuse us a little before you leave, Christian? Call us vulgar stuffed shirts?

CHRISTIAN: What makes you think you're in a position to say that, Mr. Mott? Because you think there is nothing I can do about it?

MOTT: Don't threaten me.

CHRISTIAN: I'm not threatening you.

HOW: Please, please, let me in on this.

MOTT: And I suppose you thought that if you used a frontal assault I'd be afraid to go into this little background. What happened between yourself and your wife is your own business –

CHRISTIAN: Thanks.

MOTT: But what you do where I'm personally –

HOW: Steve, isn't there a sunny side to this situation. Christian didn't tell me he was married.

MOTT: He's not.

HOW: How does a wife come into it?

MOTT: She's out of it for keeps.

HOW: You mean she threw a seven?

MOTT: That's how Christian here got into the undertaking trade.

HOW: I hope I'm not disrespectful. This is way over my head.

CHRISTIAN: Mr Mott wants to avoid unnecessary contacts with ghouls and charlatans.

MOTT: That's enough.

CHRISTIAN: I came here genuinely looking for a job to make money.

MOTT: And thought I didn't have the guts to tell you to your face that I know the whole score on you and that I'd let you just drift into my organization and blackmail my emotional life.

CHRISTIAN: Preposterous rot.

MOTT: Don't go all British with me.

HOW: Can't we galvanize this into a new situation from which it might be possible to evolve a solution. I think, despite the terrible things that have been said here, that underneath it all we're good-hearted people. That there is still something that could be considered constructive determined from –

MOTT: Determined to be a solve-it-all, are you, How? With your hired honey.

HOW: Nobody has ever talked to me like that before, not in the three years I've been working here.

MOTT: All right, all right, Howard, this is an emotional moment.

CHRISTIAN: Meanwhile I've been insulted, but Mr Mott, thank you for speaking the truth.

HOW: Now there's something we can start with. If the truth was spoken, well don't we feel the better for it. Maybe? [*Good old How, the looks as he looks from Christian to Mott.*] Hasn't the air been cleared? Maybe. Just a little. Isn't it just a case where personal history has intruded needlessly, personal lives dragged in, and personalities giving vent to feelings that have just become too emotional for words –

CHRISTIAN: I have never laid a hand on my wife. When she was deceased, Mr Mott.

MOTT: Stop being candid and embarrassing.

CHRISTIAN: It's only right that you should know. My wife's death was a blow and I said a lot of peculiar things immediately following it –

HOW: I was really proud of the impression Cornelius made on me, Steve, and I know the things you've said were tempered by some fact that could just as easily be fiction.

MOTT: Why weren't the facts laid bare, that's all, Howard, naturally what can you expect if you attempt to obscure the facts –

HOW: I'm sorry, Steve.

MOTT: Maybe I was little sudden myself, sorry to drag in your personal background like that, Christian.

CHRISTIAN: Maybe I said some things I shouldn't have said.

MOTT: Well, I guess I know I did.

HOW: We all did.

CHRISTIAN: Well, I better be going. [*Rising*]

MOTT: There's a place for you here, Christian.

HOW: Construction from confusion.

MOTT: We can use you, Christian.

HOW: Steve, I'm glad you said that.

MOTT: I'm glad I was king enough to say it.

CURTAIN

The Knockout

*

Scene One: THE BOXING-ROOM

*An arena where all is fair and square on the white mat within
the crimson ropes. And on walls pictures of fighters with muscles,
others with smiles but all standing ready to punch. Smell the
sweet sweat and fluffy warm towels. A black leather couch for
rest and folded hairy legs. On this Thursday five o'clock in this
month of May,* MIKE O'ROURKE *sits, his feet crossed on desk
by the telephone reading a newspaper as* CORNELIUS CHRIS-
TIAN *bounces in where, of course, some people fear to tread
owing to fists.*

O'ROURKE: Hey, what do you know, Cornelius.

CHRISTIAN: Hello.

O'ROURKE: Haven't seen you for a week or two. What've
you been doing?

CHRISTIAN: Making word formations.

O'ROURKE: That's good. For money?

CHRISTIAN: For money.

O'ROURKE: That's good. You think this is a free country?

CHRISTIAN: Sure.

O'ROURKE: That's good. Now let me ask you a question.

CHRISTIAN: Sure.

O'ROURKE: I was talking to my wife last night. You know

how you get into these discussions when you can't sleep. This is pretty personal, this question. You don't mind if I ask you a pretty personal question? Now promise you won't laugh if it seems funny to you.

CHRISTIAN: I won't laugh.

O'ROURKE: Do you think a girl can get pregnant sitting in the bathtub? You know. By someone taking a bath in the same tub before them. Now take your time. I don't need an answer right away, but I told my wife it can't be done. I said it was impossible.

[CHRISTIAN *pulling on the pair of yellow bag gloves, taking time to think.*]

That question needs some thought, think it over, tell me in a few days. I'll live in ignorance for a while. [O'ROURKE *spreading out newspaper, looking up and down the columns.* CHRISTIAN *rotating arms.*] Hey, tell me, Cornelius, you got a girl-friend now? You know I sort of feel you might be lonely.

CHRISTIAN: Yes.

O'ROURKE: You mean you got one.

CHRISTIAN: Yes.

O'ROURKE: Oh, that's good. Good. Sort of serious question these days, all kidding aside, you need companionship in this city. You take her out and go places?

CHRISTIAN: Once in a while.

O'ROURKE: Good. You met her around town?

CHRISTIAN: Used to know her as a kid before I went to Europe.

O'ROURKE: Childhood sweetheart. My wife was my childhood sweetheart. I never got a chance to know anything else.

[CHRISTIAN *with the quick-arm flex, shake of shoulders, bounce on toes.*]

How's the shape?

CHRISTIAN: Not bad.

O'ROURKE: You look good. Hey, you know you've created some thinking in this boxing-room since you've been back. Been interesting. Every time you go out of here and the Admiral comes in he says what's with that guy Christian, he wants to know if you've got some grudge. He says you should have stayed in Europe. I sort of told him what happened to you. But he says you're a threat to the United States. You think that's true, Cornelius?

CHRISTIAN: Yes.

O'ROURKE [*shouting*]: What? You mean I'm in the presence of a criminal? Hey, get out of here. But seriously, Cornelius. Now you tell me. What do you think about a thing like American girls?

CHRISTIAN: Whores.

O'ROURKE: Hey, you can't say a thing like that.

CHRISTIAN: Why not?

O'ROURKE: Because it ain't true. My wife's American. You mean she's a whore? That's what you said to the Admiral, he had a fit. But you know what he says? He says you're right. But he says if he ever gets you in the ring he'll kill you for some of the other things you said. He gets really burned up. He says people like you are encouragement for the Jews and Niggers to take over.

CHRISTIAN: Good.

O'ROURKE: Hey what do you mean good. [*The righteous hand on chest.*] And push the Irish out. Hey. Who do you think keeps this city honest? Wait until I tell the Admiral on you. He'll be in in a few minutes. Going to have his nails manicured. You know, the Admiral's a pretty important guy. He controls the whole harbour of New York. Could be useful, this is some harbour. Nice friendly waterfront where they're putting holes in each others heads. And what's the Admiral doing. He's in here getting his nails manicured. You think men should have their nails manicured, Cornelius? Maybe since you've been away you think we're all homosexuals in this country.

[CHRISTIAN, *that roving philosopher, sinking a few deft punches into the body-bag.*]

Hey, come on, Cornelius, you think we're all homosexuals in this country?

CHRISTIAN: Yes.

O'ROURKE: Hey, you can't say a thing like that.

CHRISTIAN: Why not?

O'ROURKE: Well, it ain't right. That's why. Now I'll tell you right away if I was homosexual how could I have the ten kids I got, now you figure that out. I don't have time to be a homosexual. You see what I mean? I go home, before I have a chance to sit down, the kids are on top of me driving me crazy. I don't even get time to be sexually normal. That's why I was wondering about this thing in the bath, getting pregnant. Now you're an intelligent guy, Cornelius, you answer me that.

CHRISTIAN: By the laws of physics, it's possible.

O'ROURKE [*shouting*]: By the laws of what? Hey, don't hand me that laws of physics stuff, can she get pregnant or not? You got to tell me because I'm arguing all night with my wife and I can't get any sleep. She even wakes me up to tell me she knows someone who got pregnant sitting in the bath. I say for Christ's sake shut up, it isn't the iceman or the milkman O.K. so she got pregnant sitting in the bath, kid's already got a christening.

CHRISTIAN: It's possible, that's all I can say.

O'ROURKE: I'm disappointed in you, Cornelius. I told my wife if anybody could settle this matter you could. That you studied physics at college. About these little bugs and germs. [*Phone rings,* O'ROURKE *picking it up.*] Bellvue Morgue, head-keeper O'Rourke speaking. No. Yeah. Yeah. O'Rourke. Speaking. The Admiral will be here any minute but you can't make this place into a beauty parlour. [*Shouting*] Women are forbidden. This is a man's domain. I'm the head boxing instructor. What do you think we are, sexually normal? That we want women around? Yeah. I'm just having a discussion here about it. You remember Cornelius Christian, who was over in Europe, all those years, yeah he's come back. Been telling us about the women over there. He says these English women have no morals at all, what about that? You don't have to marry them. They do it because they like it. What about that, huh? Sure, we'll go over there together. Sure, book on the boat. And next time you tell the Admiral that he can't bring women into this room no more, this is the last time ... We're he-men up here. [*Turns to Christian.*] That right, Cornelius, that we're he-men. [*To phone*] Yeah, now you heard me. I don't care what he wants, even if it's his ears reshaped. This is a men's club. For real men. [*To Christian*] That's right, too, huh, Cornelius. [*To phone*] Yeah, we don't want any fairies around here. Yeah, yeah, the Admiral's expected any time. You also tell the Admiral he's not kidding me when he has tea. I know what's in that pot. I asked him why he doesn't put milk in it. You're right, this city is a disgrace. [*Hangs up.*] Hey, Cornelius, I got a great idea. You know, the Admiral sees himself as one of the fighting greats. He says with his corkscrew punch he's invincible, with one of the most powerful punches around. [o'rourke *with the confidential crouch.*] And you know I think the Admiral wants to make time with this manicurist. Now I got a good idea. You know you get his goat. You answer him back. He doesn't like it. He's never heard anybody answer him back for years. Now you know what'd be good. We'll fix it up so you have a round or two. What do you say? I'll even tell him you're Jewish but you're called Christian as a disguise. How about it?

CHRISTIAN [*doing the one-foot fancy skip with rope*] : I don't know. I'm masquerading enough as it is.

O'ROURKE : Hey, it'll really be funny. Now I tell you. You fake it. Let him knock you out. It'll go over great with the manicurist. Great with the Admiral. And you've got a friend on the waterfront for life. Come on, now, how about it? Jesus, you'll be riding around with the Admiral in his yacht.

CHRISTIAN : I've taken so many beatings in various walks of life, I don't know if I'm up to an artificial one.

O'ROURKE : Come on, it'll be good. Look at it for the laughs.

CHRISTIAN : I am. It's soul destroying.

O'ROURKE : I'll be referee. You go in there, like as if you're going to kill him. A few straight lefts in the mouth, not too hard because you might put him down. Get him around the belly. Make him feel he's taking punishment and has got to pull the fight out of the bag.

CHRISTIAN: Supposing he quits?

O'ROURKE: He won't quit. Not in front of the manicurist.

CHRISTIAN: I don't know, I'm against harmful acts.

O'ROURKE: What's harmful? You call it harmful rejuvenating the Admiral. Hey, what do you want, he keeps the foreigners out of New York. Why is there so much honesty on the waterfront these days, it's the Admiral. You owe it to the country, Cornelius.

CHRISTIAN: Thanks. You just said they were shooting each other in the head on the waterfront.

O'ROURKE: But it's honest killing, can't you see the difference, the Admiral keeps it like that. [O'ROURKE *getting up to demonstrate.*] Now. A straight left to the Admiral's jaw. Then a right on the belly. Leave yourself open. He throws a counter punch and you go down. Let him hit you at the end of the round.

CHRISTIAN: I think it's against my principles to make anyone a victim like that.

O'ROURKE: Hey, what do you mean, victim? We're all victims. Hey, you used to be one of the toughest little fighters I ever saw around here before you went to Europe. What happened?

CHRISTIAN: O.K. I'll spar with the Admiral.

O'ROURKE: Great. [O'ROURKE's *long surveying look at Christian.*] You know now, you've changed Cornelius. You used to be a wild guy here.

[CHRISTIAN *throwing a few fancy left and right uppercuts with some dignity.*]

You think it's because there are no moral values in Europe. That maybe you had to struggle against it. You know, all you hear from people coming back is how they got cheated, robbed, and gyped, even in these quaint little English villages. I try to tell them everybody is gyping you, only here they do it right in front of your face.

[*Turning to opening door,* ADMIRAL *entering, white bundle of bathrobe, towel around neck, the new boxing-shoes, with nice rim of white sweat sock over tops, pair of boxing-gloves strung over arm.*]

Hey, it's the Admiral, how are you, Admiral? Come in and sit down. Cornelius Christian's here.

ADMIRAL: So I see.

O'ROURKE: What's a matter, Admiral, Christian's not a bad guy, he's a little naughty with his free thinking or something he learned over in Europe.

ADMIRAL: Don't talk to me about Europe. I'm a taxpayer.

O'ROURKE: We're all taxpayers, Admiral.

ADMIRAL [*looking in Christian's direction as he does shoulder rotation under robe and sits on arse*]: I don't want my tax money supporting people like him, coming in here. Criticizing this country.

O'ROURKE: He only said American women are whores.

ADMIRAL: And it makes me very sad to have to agree with him.

O'ROURKE: Hear that, Cornelius? What the Admiral says. You agree on something. Hey, wait a minute. Where do I come into it, hey what about my wife. You calling my wife a whore? Hey, you can't say that. She's a mother of six kids.

ADMIRAL: I'm not talking about wives.

O'ROURKE: My wife's a woman.

ADMIRAL [*while* CHRISTIAN *curls a few hooks into the body-bag. Admiral in Christian's direction*]: He ought to get married, knock some responsibility into him.

O'ROURKE [*finger quickly to lips, hand admonishing quiet to Admiral. Changing subject*]: Admiral, what's the idea of making this into a beauty saloon every afternoon?

ADMIRAL: It protects me from the evil atmosphere.

O'ROURKE: Come on, Admiral, don't be like that. We're just a big family. Enter into the free spirit here.

ADMIRAL: What free spirit?

O'ROURKE: None of this bitter talk this afternoon, Admiral. We all want to be happy here. You're trying to depress us because you can't adjust to life. Cornelius has a lot of interesting ideas.

[ADMIRAL *grunts.*]

O'ROURKE: Now how can I talk with you like this. He's been telling me a lot of real fascinating things. Why right over there in London they've got whores all over the place and in all the houses. Now would you let whores on the waterfront, Admiral, that's all we want to know today.

ADMIRAL: Don't talk rot.

O'ROURKE: That ain't rot. Don't you think it's better that we get physical enjoyment without having to spend the rest of our lives raising the results? We ought to let some of these English women over here. You control the immigration, Admiral. Let them in. Christian told me only a couple of weeks ago that American women don't even excite him. Only English girls excite him. Right, Cornelius?

ADMIRAL: Why doesn't he go back there? I already pay too much taxes keeping people on relief in this city.

CHRISTIAN [*punching bag*]: You deserve to pay more taxes.

ADMIRAL: Why, God damn it, do you pay taxes?

CHRISTIAN: I live in Limbo.

ADMIRAL: That's the kind of smart talk they learn these days. I wouldn't mind having you on one of my ships.

CHRISTIAN: Lot of admirals have felt that way.

ADMIRAL: God damn free thinking. [*The disgruntled pause.*] Free fornication.

O'ROURKE: Hey, what's this about free fornication? Watch that word in here. Bad language is forbidden.

ADMIRAL: Just a day on one of my ships.

O'ROURKE: Hey, Cornelius's been in the navy, Admiral.

ADMIRAL: Children's navy.

O'ROURKE: He had a stripe.

ADMIRAL: On his ass.

O'ROURKE: Hey. Even I had two stripes. You can't insult officers, Admiral.

ADMIRAL: Who gave you your stripes?

O'ROURKE [*snapping to attention and salute, a nice flourish of tatty silk robe*]: Hello, captain of the ship. Away all anchors. Full astern. Secure all bulkheads. Off to the beach fighting Amphibians. [O'ROURKE'S *nice rendition of anchors aweigh.*] How's that, Admiral?

ADMIRAL: I come in here and have to listen to all this claptrap.

CHRISTIAN: Jews and Niggers I hear are taking all the seats on the subway. I suggest burning in oil.

ADMIRAL: That's the kind of thing I'd expect you to say.

O'ROURKE: Forward with the Irish.

ADMIRAL: Goddam trash.

O'ROURKE: Hey, watch that about the Irish.

ADMIRAL [*levelling the authoritative finger at Christian*]: But you better understand that you can't say that kind of thing here.

CHRISTIAN: I've said it.

[*My goodness, the silent fury of that Admiral.*]

O'ROURKE: Now why don't you two be friends and instead of wasting a lot of hot air on each other, use this room the way it's supposed to be used. [*Shouting*] For the manly sport. The art of self-defence.

ADMIRAL: I'm expecting my manicurist.

O'ROURKE: Now, Admiral, how many times do I have to tell you to stop using this place like that?

ADMIRAL: When you stop using it as a place of business I'll start using it for the manly sport.

O'ROURKE: How am I going to sell my antiques if I don't keep in touch with my store? Got a great thing, I got them drilling holes in the picture frames to make it look like real worms been in the wood. Want to buy an old master, Admiral? Come on, for the dining-room on your yacht. Cheap.

ADMIRAL: Forgeries from some back room in the Bronx.

O'ROURKE: Genuine. Out of real castles in Germany.

ADMIRAL: What do I care, maybe you've got a back room in Brooklyn.

O'ROURKE: You heard him, Cornelius, trying to discredit my business.

ADMIRAL: Have you ever been in an art gallery?

O'ROURKE: What for? I do all right. Got two guys with doctorates in the history of art. I always say if they got degrees it stops them stealing.

[*Knock on door. Shouting*]

Come in. To the nest of vipers.

GENTLE [*tray in hand, peeking in door*]: Oh, I thought this was the boxing-room, sorry.

O'ROURKE: Hey, come back, it is. Can't you hear us fighting in here.?

GENTLE: I'm looking for Admiral Fuller.

O'ROURKE [*pointing the accusing finger*]: There he is.

[GENTLE *enters shyly.*]

ADMIRAL: Don't listen to this man. Come in.

[*Hesitating* GENTLE.]

I won't bite you. Come in. Put the tray over here.

GENTLE [*apprehensive looks from face to face*]: Yes, sir.

ADMIRAL: That's it. Right over here. Sit down.

[O'ROURKE *making mock motions behind Admiral's back to Christian.*]

Make yourself comfortable. What's your name?

GENTLE: Miss Gentle.

ADMIRAL: Your first name?

GENTLE: Gertrude.

ADMIRAL: Good. Now I'll have some of that tea, Gertrude. You don't mind my calling you Gertrude?

GENTLE: No, sir.

ADMIRAL: With just one lump of sugar.

GENTLE: Yes, sir.

ADMIRAL: I'm sick of being called sir, call me anything but sir. Makes me feel I'm some sort of freak.

GENTLE: Yes. Of course. I mean, sorry. I mean –

ADMIRAL: Forget it.

O'ROURKE: Now, Admiral, none of that. I know what you've got in that pot.

ADMIRAL: I'm having a lump of sugar in it.

O'ROURKE: Put milk in it too.

ADMIRAL: I don't like milk. Tell him, Gertrude, what this is. What did you ask for from the dining-room?

O'ROURKE: Bar.

ADMIRAL: Didn't you say the Admiral's tea?

O'ROURKE: Whisky.

GENTLE: Yes, I did.

ADMIRAL: And isn't this what they gave you?

GENTLE: Yes.

O'ROURKE: Put milk in it.

ADMIRAL: I have this young woman here to testify.

[GENTLE *pouring this particularly strong tea.*]

O'ROURKE: Put milk in it.

ADMIRAL: I happen to prefer my tea plain.

O'ROURKE: A hundred proof. What about that, Cornelius? Isn't this a disgrace? This a temple of athletic achievement. What an example! I better go back to reading about today's murders.

GENTLE: I've got my things here, sir, I mean no, sir, I mean, Admiral. Shall I start on your free hand?

ADMIRAL: Just put back some of this tea first.

GENTLE: Of course.

[O'ROURKE *from paper, a mocking finger at the Admiral.*]

ADMIRAL [*quickly lowering back handsomely the tea-tinted*

firewater]: Ah, that's better. Could do with a crumpet. [*To Gentle*] Tell me, have you been long here at the club?

GENTLE: Just a week.

ADMIRAL: Thought I hadn't seen your face before. How would you like to get the Admiral's tea tomorrow too? [*Towards O'Rourke*] I'll be having it up at the squash courts.

O'ROURKE: Not good enough for you down here, Admiral? Hey, you watch him, Gertrude, don't let him get you in one of those lonely squash courts.

ADMIRAL: Don't mind him. Won't have to tolerate this talk upstairs where people have better manners.

GENTLE: I don't mind.

ADMIRAL: Well, you should.

O'ROURKE: Hey, Admiral, before you have your nails done why don't you have a little spar around the ring with Cornelius?

CHRISTIAN [*that lonely left-out shadow-boxing man*]: I think I'd rather not.

O'ROURKE: Come on now, Cornelius, the Admiral won't hurt you. That's true, Admiral, you don't hold any grudge against Cornelius, do you? Even though he wants to string up a few of the dark-complexioned citizens. Sorry, Gertrude, just a little discussion we were having.

[ADMIRAL *grunts.*]

GENTLE: I'll just get started. [GERTRUDE *making preparations for the manicure.*]

O'ROURKE: See, Cornelius, the Admiral promises not to use anything lethal. Now, Admiral, the corkscrew punch is illegal, now you understand that. I don't want any-body hurt while I'm running this boxing-room.

ADMIRAL: It behoves me –

O'ROURKE: Behoove, behoove, behoove, what do you mean behoove? Big words are banned here, all I want is your solemn promise not to use the corkscrew punch, never mind the behoove business. [*To Christian*] There now, Cornelius, got the Admiral's solemn promise.

CHRISTIAN: I think I'd rather not. [*Doing the drill of the desultory left and right hooks, albeit neatly executed.*]

O'ROURKE: Hey, come on, Cornelius. What more can you ask for than the Admiral's solemn promise not to touch you with the corkscrew, which I now ban for all time from this boxing-room? Miss Gentle is a witness, aren't you, Miss Gentle, a witness?

[*Shy nod of* GENTLE *head.*]

There now. And you also have the solemn oath of O'Rourke. [*Hand raised on Boy Scout's honour.*] Now you're not going to use that corkscrew [*pointing finger*], Admiral.

ADMIRAL: Don't be preposterous, when have I ever struck a man who couldn't defend himself?

O'ROURKE: There you are, Cornelius. Go in there with the Admiral. You'll get some pointers. Come on, before he has his fingers done.

CHRISTIAN [*using the sad slouch to the slaughter*]: O.K. All right.

ADMIRAL: To me sport is give and take. I don't want to mix it with someone who can't defend himself.

O'ROURKE: Cornelius is no cripple, Admiral. But if you hold the corkscrew in check nobody is going to get hurt.

ADMIRAL: I can never promise to keep the corkscrew in check.

O'ROURKE: But you just promised.

ADMIRAL: It's an instinctive punch with me. And comes out of nowhere. I don't even know how I do it myself.

O'ROURKE: It's pretty obvious, Admiral, where it comes from, look at the way you're set up, like a kid of twenty.

ADMIRAL [*running up ensign of health, little expansion of steel chest*]: I keep myself in shape. Every ship that goes to sea under my command is in a rigorous state of health.

O'ROURKE: You're telling me. Who put them in shape? Me. I was your athletic commander.

ADMIRAL: Commander of the bar.

O'ROURKE [*to the salute*]: Forgive me, Captain.

ADMIRAL: I keep myself in shape.

O'ROURKE: Miss Gentle would you know, by looking at him, that the Admiral has one of the most lethal punches ever seen in the ring?

[ADMIRAL'*s agonizing modesty.*]

Naturally he doesn't like it talked about. But you can't deny it, Admiral.

ADMIRAL: I don't deny it. I prefer it be known. Anyone entering the ring with me knows the risk he runs by doing so.

O'ROURKE [*the supplication*]: I just finished, you heard me twice, Admiral, telling Cornelius you weren't going to use it. You wouldn't be that kind of sportsman. I mean we're sportsmen here, aren't we?

ADMIRAL: Why don't you buy a new robe?

O'ROURKE: Hey, what's the matter with my robe?

ADMIRAL: This young lady here, I don't want her to think that we boxers have no sartorial elegance.

O'ROURKE: Where do you get off with that word sartorial? Speak English. Cornelius there, he's got no elegance neither. He told me it was a cultured European touch to wear rags.

ADMIRAL: That's what American womenhood have to look forward to with his type. What's this country coming to?

O'ROURKE [*shouting*]: Protect yourself, Cornelius. Don't let him talk to you like that.

[CHRISTIAN'*s smile.*]

Admiral, you going to box with Cornelius or aren't you?

ADMIRAL: If he's prepared I'm prepared.

O'ROURKE: O.K., on with the gloves. [O'ROURKE *to Christian to help on with his gloves.*]

ADMIRAL: Would you give me a hand with these, Gertrude, tie them tight around the wrists, no flying laces.

O'ROURKE: Now remember, no hitting on the break. No rabbit punches. I'm going to watch for any foul blows in this.

ADMIRAL: Don't tell me the rules.

O'ROURKE: I want a clean fight. Especially with a lady present. Now let's see. [O'ROURKE *looking up at clock.*] Set the bell on the clock. [*Bell rings.*] O.K., at the next bell come out fighting.

[ADMIRAL *derobing, poor old* CHRISTIAN *a little roughshod underneath, but even in these hard times faces life with a flourish. The two preposterous contenders slip through the velvet ropes. Repair to respective corners and each make a visit to the rosin in the neutral corner like real pros. And they wait for the bell.* O'ROURKE *naturally is at the tea pot on the couch next to Gentle.*]

And now I'll pour myself a nice cup of tea if you don't mind, Admiral.

ADMIRAL: Get away from that teapot.

O'ROURKE [*pouring and sipping*]: Well, what do you know, it is tea.

ADMIRAL: You scoundrel.

O'ROURKE: Well I'll just help myself to a little tea. [*To Gertrude*] This is what the Admiral trains on, it's what gives him the corkscrew. We know where you got that corkscrew punch now, Admiral. Cornelius, you duck when it comes.

CHRISTIAN: If the Admiral should like to use the corkscrew it's quite all right with me.

O'ROURKE: That's the way, Cornelius. We don't want any withholding. But, Admiral, if you use that corkscrew, make sure it's at half power. Now as the referee of this sparring match that's an order. Hey wait a minute. [O'ROURKE *goes to wall, takes head protector.*] Just get this on. We've all got the raging bull in us and Cornelius you've got your future ahead of you. It fit?

CORNELIUS: Thanks. [*Bong the gong.*]

O'ROURKE: O.K., now go to it and may the best man win.

GENTLE [*Gertrude, that gentle, disconcerted*]: They're not going to hurt each other.

O'ROURKE [*the whisper*]: Just humouring the Admiral along, he couldn't break a spider's web.

GENTLE: Oh, this is just a joke.

O'ROURKE: Just a joke. That's it, Cornelius, keep well

away from that right. Circle to your right. Now, Admiral, remember what I told you.

ADMIRAL: Shut up.

O'ROURKE: Hey, I got to tell my fighter what to do. Watch it, Cornelius, he's sizing up your style.

[CORNELIUS CHRISTIAN *briefly turning and running*.] [*Outright*.] Hey, Cornelius, take your beating like a man. Don't go yellow.

ADMIRAL: He's backing away. I can't hit him.

O'ROURKE: What do you expect if you're going to use the corkscrew? Only fair evasion. Christian has some of the best footwork I've ever seen. Hard man to hit. Be careful of Christian's right, Admiral. He's handy with the under-the-heart punch.

ADMIRAL: I'm not worried.

O'ROURKE: Are you all right, Cornelius?

CHRISTIAN: I'm fine. Just warming up.

O'ROURKE: Keep your gloves up, that's it, take his left on your shoulder, circle to your right, keep out of the way of the Admiral's wine punch.

ADMIRAL: Very funny.

O'ROURKE: I don't want any unconscious bodies in this boxing-room. I'm watching you, Admiral.

ADMIRAL: Why don't you shut up?

O'ROURKE: I'm responsible for all lives in here. This is just like a ship.

ADMIRAL: He's doing all right. He doesn't need your shipboard advice. He's got a nice little punch. Just caught me. [*To Christian*] Nice punch.

CHRISTIAN: Thanks.

ADMIRAL: Only tell me if I'm hurting you.

71

CHRISTIAN: You're not hurting me.

O'ROURKE: Don't start to become friends. Hit him, Cornelius.

ADMIRAL [*to Christian*]: Sure I'm not hurting you?

CHRISTIAN: Not a bit.

ADMIRAL: Good. I like to punch clean and crisp. I like a good fight. It does not behove me to do permanent damage.

CHRISTIAN: That's O.K.

ADMIRAL: Just tell me when you've had enough. I like a good workout, gets up a sweat. Sorry that was a low punch.

O'ROURKE: Now watch him, Cornelius, he's sneaky. Watch for the flexing of his right knee, only don't let him hit you one when you're looking. There, he just gave you his feeler punch.

ADMIRAL: Enough out of you, O'Rourke.

O'ROURKE [*to tea kettle*]: Just try a little more of your tea, skipper. [*To Miss Gentle*] Two fine men out there, don't you think, Miss Gentle? Two real sportsmen.

GENTLE: Yes.

O'ROURKE: Truly the manly art. Have a little spot of tea, Miss Gentle, plenty of cups.

GENTLE: Thank you, but isn't it against club rules for me to have anything? I think so.

O'ROURKE: I rule here.

GENTLE [*the smile of Gentle*]: Oh.

O'ROURKE [*pouring, shouting*]: Hit him. Hit him. Right in the beer belly, Cornelius. That's it, you're doing fine. [*To Gentle*] Sorry for the language, but you know how it is.

GENTLE: Oh, it's all right by me. [*Tea to lips.*] Oh, my goodness. [*A slight ladylike spluttering out. If only all women were as nice as Miss Gentle.*]

O'ROURKE: Oh, sorry, Miss Gentle. [*Wiping with towel.*]

GENTLE: It's all right. I really thought it was tea.

ADMIRAL: Ruffian.

[*In that arena, a general slowing down of huffing puffing contestants.*]

O'ROURKE: Jew Fight. Let's see some action. [*A pirouette to a moment of Boccherini minuet.*] He's wide open, Cornelius, for a left to the nose. That's it, get him before he tries the corkscrew. Punish him around the body. Now a left. Hook him, hook him. Now. Watch it, Cornelius, that stance he's using is deadly. Duck.

[CHRISTIAN *ducking,* ADMIRAL'*s punch passing over head.*]

[O'ROURKE *leaping to feet, shouting.*] I saw it, I saw it, that was it, Admiral. I saw you use the corkscrew. At full power. I saw you. You know it's fatal at close quarters.

ADMIRAL: You stay out of this and stop drinking any more of my whisky.

O'ROURKE: You admit it. Well I saw you and don't tell me I didn't. I'm ashamed. If I hadn't told Cornelius to duck we'd be picking up his head from over there on Wall street. [*To Christian*] Weight well forward on the balls of the feet, Cornelius – that's the only adequate defence against the corkscrew. [*To Admiral*] That's how you run the waterfront. [*To Miss Gentle*] See, Miss. Men who have unlimited physical resources and who don't know their own strength ought to be stopped using it. Good mind to stop the fight.

GENTLE [*getting to feet, hand to lips*]: Oh, my goodness.

O'ROURKE: Hey, you hit him with the corkscrew.

[CORNELIUS *flat, spread-eagled on canvas.*]

Now don't say you didn't, you hit him with the corkscrew. I saw you do it.

GENTLE: Is he all right?

O'ROURKE [*winking*]: Look at him, you've knocked him right out, I told you not to use the corkscrew. You don't know your own strength. I told you.

ADMIRAL [*that mountain of power, slayer of all women, taking off gloves, as he crosses ring with the slow swagger*]: Ahem. [*Throat cleared.*]

O'ROURKE: What's the idea, Admiral, hey, we've got to pick him up, just don't leave him like that.

GENTLE: Can I do something. Get something, some smelling salts. Medical attendant in the hall has some.

O'ROURKE [*to Admiral*]: Hey, he needs artificial respiration, Admiral.

ADMIRAL: It was merely a tap. Leave him there. He's had that coming for a long time. Knock some sense in him.

[O'ROURKE *smiling to Gentle from behind Admiral.*]

Won't be coming into this boxing-room again talking a lot of damn nonsense.

O'ROURKE: Well, Admiral, let me shake your hand. Now don't give me the dynamite shake. Just let me shake. Didn't want to tell you, but you know that's the first time Cornelius Christian's ever hit the deck. Didn't want to say anything. But he was middle Atlantic champion before he went to Europe, seven straight knock-outs. Seven straight.

ADMIRAL [*robe on, patting himself both-handed on ribs*]: He had me guessing. Just for a few seconds. I've often refrained from using the corkscrew even when I've seen an inviting opening. But that kid's too smart for his own good. Not enough red blood these days.

O'ROURKE: Yeah.

ADMIRAL: That's the trouble.

O'ROURKE: You bet, Admiral.

ADMIRAL: When I took my first ship to sea I used to skip rope around the quarter deck for two hours before breakfast. That's how I got that stomach you call a beer barrel. Barrel of nails. Give it a punch. You young girl. Try it. Go on. Don't be shy. There. See?

[*Gentle punch.*]

O'ROURKE: Armour plating. Bet Christian knew he was hitting something when he tried a few on that.

ADMIRAL: That's what a clean life does.

O'ROURKE: Cleaned your teapot for you, Admiral.

ADMIRAL: Miss Gentle, take no notice of him.

GENTLE: Oh, I'm not. [*To O'Rourke, looking at poor Christian prostrate*] But he's all right, isn't he?

ADMIRAL [*taking the Gentle arm*]: My girl, it's nice to see someone like you so concerned. Gives your eyes a nice look. But I assure you he'll come around and be all right in a few days. [*Rotation of head for the new fields to conquer.*] Well, that was a good afternoon's exercise.

GENTLE [*looking back*]: I just thought I saw him twitch.

ADMIRAL: Little corkscrew never does anybody any permanent harm. It's scientific. The glove rotates as the punch leaves and when it lands, quicker than the human eye can see, it gives extra penetrating force. I developed it after years of experiment, based on the rifling in a gun barrel.

O'ROURKE: Rename it the sixteen-inch shell punch, Admiral.

ADMIRAL: Had enough of your suggestions, for one afternoon. Well, Miss Gentle, rather Gertrude [*offering of arm that threw the corkscrew*], I think we'll proceed to the baths department, to a more salubrious atmosphere where we can get down to having these nails done. [*To O'Rourke.*] I think he's been there long enough, throw some water on him. [*Moving out.*] I don't want to embarrass him by being around. Come along, Gertrude, we'll give this Christian some privacy to recover in.

GENTLE [*to O'Rourke*]: Sure you don't want any smelling salts?

O'ROURKE: Wouldn't help. Felled like a tree. But Cornelius took it like a man. But you shouldn't have done it, Admiral.

ADMIRAL: Do him good. But no hard feelings. Tell him I'll be in the eleventh floor lounge later, buy him a drink. In the ring I may be a killer, but outside I believe in behaving like a normal human being. Any born boxer would have done what I did when he saw his opening.

O'ROURKE: Your conscience is clear, Admiral. I can tell you mean what you say. I think maybe Cornelius did have it coming to him. Like a lot of guys who feel this country could do with changing. And that our wives are out to get us for alimony and sell themselves.

ADMIRAL: I think that kind of talk is out of turn with Gertrude present here.

GERTRUDE: But I like men who hate women.

O'ROURKE: Hey, get that, Admiral. If Christian was only conscious he would have liked that remark.

ADMIRAL: I think it's time to have my nails done, Miss Gentle. Down to the baths.

O'ROURKE [*at door*]: So long, Miss Gentle. Bye, Admiral, and watch that corkscrew, that's banned from now on. [O'ROURKE *turning now to ring*] That was great, Cornelius. Why the Admiral will be inviting you down to his boat, get free rides all around the harbour. I have to laugh, that was really good acting, for a second I really thought it looked like he knocked you cold. [*Getting closer.*] Hey, Cornelius, what's the matter. The Admiral's gone, get up. [*Touching head that rolls.*] Hey, Cornelius. [*Shouting after Gentle and Admiral.*] Hey, come back, bring the smelling salts.

CURTAIN

ACT FOUR

Peach Shoes

*

Scene One: THE RESTAURANT

This old but lavish eatery with its factory windows. A white covered table in the sunken garden. In June and waiters go to and fro, high nosed and sniffing and brow lifting. CORNELIUS CHRISTIAN and CHARLOTTE GRAVES step down steps and a waiter disdaining, points them to a table during this late high sunned afternoon. Pots of deep grass wave white and warm. They walk and sit at chairs, iron, white, and filigree. Cornelius sad and silent and touches the silver salt and pepper things. Charlotte bowed, her straw wide hat on her haystack hair. The sad late afternoon begins.

CHRISTIAN [*a proffered hand half across the table*]: But didn't you know, that peach is really the snazz.

GRAVES: No, I didn't know.

CHRISTIAN: I'm starting a fashion.

GRAVES [*straw-haired head up*]: But they looked at us.

CHRISTIAN: I thought you were so tickled pink to go out with me.

GRAVES: I was. I am.

CHRISTIAN: I feel smooth in these shoes. I walked along the highway this afternoon really feeling big time.

Policemen were parked sitting in their car, in their nice blue uniforms waiting for speeders. They just looked at me from behind their sunglasses. Ha, ha, you've never seen such bellies in blue. They saw my shoes. And I just looked back at them with that air, that I know somebody who knows somebody who's something and you better watch out. I made no impression but I wasn't arrested. I passed by, putting an extra inch on my chest, and smiled. [*Shooting a shoe forward.*] I am proud of these shoes.

GRAVES: We're just sitting here. [*Her head down.*] And nothing is happening. They're just ignoring us.

[*The light gay music and laughter from another room*] And listen, all those other people in furs in the other room. The men all had black shoes and black ties and white shirts. They were all formal. And the waiters were hurrying around them.

[*Waiter returning across the sunken garden-room.*] See.

CHRISTIAN [*raising a hand, two delicate snaps of thumb and index. Ignored*]: I see. [*A supplicant hand to foot.*] My own toes are inside. Which I'm wiggling at the moment. This place was just a factory once. Way out in the woods. They had Alsatian dogs to nibble at the unruly. Also a policeman patrolling with a night-stick up and down between the tables.

GRAVES: This is our first big night-out together. I'm dressed in the best I have. This belonged to my grandmother. She was married in it, it's an heirloom.

[CHRISTIAN *mumchance.* CHARLOTTE GRAVES *reaches out for his hand.*]

Don't think, please, that I mind, it's only that we're here. And I don't want everyone just to notice us.

CHRISTIAN: You're a kid, Charlotte.

GRAVES: I'm not a kid. I feel awful. And I can't help it.

CHRISTIAN: You shouldn't let these waiters scare you.

GRAVES: We could have been taken into that other room where they have the music and dancing. And there's nothing in here.

[CHRISTIAN *turns swiftly to the lurking waiter at the pantry door, who swiftly turns and goes into the kitchen beyond.*]

You see what they're doing to us? We don't even have menus.

CHRISTIAN [*upturned palms*]: Doubts about my taste are evident. Do you want me to hide my shoes.

GRAVES: It's too late now. They won't come to us.

CHRISTIAN: We'll wait. Smile.

GRAVES: I can't.

CHRISTIAN: You have such a real mouth. And such large teeth. And such a worried frown. Face my shoes.

[GRAVES *with mumchance.*]

Remember the summer when we were kids. [CHRISTIAN *rubbing hands.*] The Labour Day picnic and parade. I saw you coming out of your house, in a white silk blouse, and the same haystack hair. You gave me the biggest hello I've ever had in my life. [CHRISTIAN *looks up in air.*] I can still hear it. It made me even march in the parade, no, I'm lying. I skulked behind the trees, stealing ice-cream while the citizens of my country marched. You're still such a kid. My shoes are in bad taste. [*Shouting.*] My shoes are in bad taste.

GRAVES: Please. [*Worried appearance of two waiters.*] Please, I don't mind your pink shoes.

CHRISTIAN: Peach.

GRAVES: Peach. But should we go?

CHRISTIAN [*fighter for freedom*]: No.

GRAVES: Can't we ask for something then?

CHRISTIAN: For them to forgive us. And me for my shoes that cost eighteen dollars.

GRAVES: Just so that they come and go from the table.

CHRISTIAN: Alas I reckon I do lower the tone.

GRAVES: Cornelius –

CHRISTIAN: I've got such a beautiful name.

GRAVES: We come from the same background. Our backgrounds are medium and middle, we can't be sure we're right, that's all I'm saying. The better people are right.

CHRISTIAN: We're not the better people?

GRAVES: We may be better than some people. But we're not the best people, that's all I'm saying.

CHRISTIAN: You were so tan and lovely at the Labour Day parade.

GRAVES: I just don't want all the best people thinking we can't be just like them.

CHRISTIAN: I took you out on your first date. Bought you a soda after the movies. I remember distinctly my aplomb. As I said to the candy-store man, two pineapple please. I was his customer. He welcomed me.

GRAVES: Because you were nice.

CHRISTIAN: What am I now?

GRAVES: You're different. You're not the same Cornelius Christian I used to know.

CHRISTIAN: Who am I?

GRAVES: You're just not the same as you were. Before you went to Europe.

[CHRISTIAN *performing a close examination of his person.*] And before you –

CHRISTIAN: Got married.

GRAVES: Please. [*Looking round.*] They'll start to listen to us.

CHRISTIAN: Good.

GRAVES: You said I was so tan and lovely at the Labour Day parade. You don't think that now.

CHRISTIAN: You're still an apple I'd love to eat.

GRAVES: I haven't been swimming yet, I guess. Living in the city I don't get a chance. That's why tonight to come to the country and all.

CHRISTIAN [*picking up the silver cellar, pounding it on the table, shouting*]: Service, service.

GRAVES: That's the last thing I want you to do.

CHRISTIAN: I am merely asking for service. [*Shouting and pounding.*] Service. [*Peeking heads of waiters.*]

GRAVES: Now you have ruined the whole evening. No one has ever behaved in my presence like this before.

CHRISTIAN: Do you want me to leave?

GRAVES: You know I don't want you to leave.

CHRISTIAN: Well that's just fine.

GRAVES: No, it isn't fine. You're being conceited.

CHRISTIAN: You do want me to leave. Do you? Tell me. Do you want me to leave?

GRAVES [*shouting*]: Yes. Leave.

[CHRISTIAN *a movement of the lips, rising slowly, steps back, hesitates for reprieve. None. Gently pushing chair beneath the table. Proceeds slowly past Head waiter and*

*Waiter, who straighten backs to look down their high
sniffing noses at the peach tootsies of Cornelius Christian.
Up the steps Christian goes. Stopping at top to speak.
Waiters gingerly into kitchen. And Christian's eyes upon
Charlotte Graves, an anguished bent head. Christian exits.
Waiters pop out. Wait and whisper.* CHARLOTTE *looks
up the empty stairs. Bites her lips. And with pinkly-
coloured nail she touches the table things one by one. Looks
up again and around in this unfriendly world and the
waiters turn ashamed away. They take trays held over
shoulders towards that room where the gay and better
people live and laugh in crowded lavishment. A tide of
laughter and Charlotte turns, but it's not for her. She takes
up her straw, wide hat and puts it back on her straw hair.
A mouse alone. This open field. The* HEAD WAITER
*comes. Stands a hovering hawk. She looks up the black
shoes, trousers, to the white shirt and face.*]

WAITER: Would madam like some service for herself?
[GRAVES *shakes head – no.*]

Isn't there anything I can get madam? Like water. [*Shakes
head – no.*] An omelette? Crêpe suzette? Steak? [*Shakes
head – no.*] Would madam, then, like some explanation?
[*Shakes head – yes.*] We have certain unwritten rules.
Which it is understood people understand before they
come here. We do not mind when persons come where
this is not their natural habitat. We try to make them
feel at home and not as if they don't belong.

[CHARLOTTE *putting a hand to her forehead.*]

Maybe madam would like to be seated in the other
room? [*Shakes head – no.*] I don't want to hurt madam's
feelings but should madam be interested in my advice

I would say that he is not your kind. We expected him to leave. But we have a lot of experience in telling who is who. No gentleman would treat a lady the way he has treated you. He shouted for service.

CHARLOTTE: Because you wouldn't give us any.

WAITER: Oh, no, nothing like that.

CHARLOTTE: It was like that.

WAITER: If madam will permit me, we get lots like him. We know his kind well. Distinctly from the other side of the tracks.

CHARLOTTE: He's from my side.

WAITER: Look, we know you feel you owe him some kind of loyalty, but boy I wouldn't like to have to count the trains on the tracks between you and him. Girl like you could meet people of top quality. And really frequent places like this.

CHARLOTTE: I wouldn't want to.

WAITER: You're a hard kid to please, you know that. You don't mind if I say one or two very personal things. You know, I can tell you're a girl who comes from real nice people. Only. Don't take what I'm going to tell you wrong. But that dress you're wearing looks like it belonged to your grandmother.

[CHARLOTTE *turning head away*.]

I'm just trying to help you out. You don't want to misunderstand me. I'm just joking about the dress. O.K. I think it suits you. But a kid with your looks wants to show them off. Guy with a lot of dough would like to be seen with you. I'm not saying you looked like you stepped out of an antique shop.

CHARLOTTE: You are.

WAITER: No, no. You got real good looks. And tone. Excuse me for saying it, but that guy was a greaseball. [CHARLOTTE *bent.*] Hey, I said something. Look, you're going to cry. Don't cry. I said something. I did, didn't I? Just tell me what I said. [*Motions to other Waiter and* CHARLIE *comes. They stand towels over arms.*] Charlie, what am I going to do?

CHARLIE: Leave the kid alone. [*To Graves*] Here, kid. [*An offering of towel.*] Help you mop up.

[GRAVES *opens her bag for hanky.*]

Don't worry, kid, it's all right. Nobody's going to hurt you. [*To Fritz*] What you do this to the kid for. She's crying.

FRITZ: It was that guy.

CHARLIE: So what? No need to make the kid cry.

FRITZ: I was trying to steer her straight.

CHARLIE: I suppose you know just how to straighten everybody out. [*A hand towards Charlotte.*] What the hell, it's none of your business.

FRITZ: She came in here with a guy who was a phoney. I could tell a mile off.

CHARLIE: So what? Everybody in this place is phoney.

FRITZ [*apocryphal hand lifted*]: You call Mr Van Hearse and his party in there phoney?

CHARLIE: Yeah. I call them phoney. What the hell is he but some guy who makes rubber goods.?

FRITZ: Don't say that in front of women. Mr Van Hearse is a public benefactor.

CHARLIE: Don't start giving him titles. He makes rubber goods.

FRITZ: You said that once, you don't have to say it again.

CHARLIE: I like the sound.

FRITZ: I'm busy. We better clear this table.

CHARLIE: Why don't you leave the kid?

FRITZ: We got to clear this table.

CHARLIE: Who's coming? We don't need this table.

FRITZ: Who gives the orders around here?

CHARLIE: I'm just telling you to give the kid a break.

FRITZ: And I'm giving you an order to clear the table. Understand English?

CHARLIE: Thought you were trying to help this kid.

FRITZ: She still thinks the guy who walked out on her is something. When he's a phoney. A phoney cheapskate.

CHARLIE: Look cut it out, you're really hurting the kid's feelings.

FRITZ: Any kid go out with a guy like that deserves to have her feelings hurt.

CHARLIE [*the pointing finger held high, punctuating*]: Look. I don't care if I've got to take orders from you. But you're not going to upset this kid any more. Because I'll slug you. That's English. Understand it?

FRITZ: You touch me and you're fired.

CHARLIE: And you say one more thing to this kid and I'll slug you right out of the window up there.

FRITZ: Tough.

CHARLIE: About this. Yeah.

FRITZ: We'll see.

CHARLIE: You see.

FRITZ: I'll see. Don't worry.

CHARLIE: Go ahead. I'm worried.

FRITZ: You just clear that table like I said, that's all.

CHARLIE: And you just leave this kid alone, that's all.

FRITZ: Clear the table, that's all. [*Leaving with the backward step.*]

CHARLIE [*to Graves*]: Sorry, kid, I got to do this. Don't worry. This happens to everybody, if not every day at least once in their life. Don't mind that guy, this joint's a dump, believe me. We just had to give your boy-friend the cold shoulder because the owner thinks he's going to make this dive into a toney establishment if he makes a few people think they're not wanted. [*A slow popping of table's items on to his tray.*] Some hope he's got. I know it's kind of late to say these things. But look, I didn't have anything personal against your boy-friend. [*Picking up tall glass vase, three roses, puts tray on table, snaps off a rose.*] Here. Here's a rose.

GRAVES: Thank you.

CHARLIE: Look, I tell you what. Why don't me and you go somewhere. I'm quitting this job right now. I know of a swell place just a couple of miles down the highway. Nice floor show, take your mind off this. What about it, huh?

GRAVES: Thanks but – [*Shakes head – no.*]

CHARLIE: Look, believe me, he's gone. Your boy-friend's not coming back. He's run out on you and left you here. All alone. [*Picks up tray.*] Come on. What have you got to lose? Think it over. We could go to a nice quiet place if you want. With soft lights. Then I'll take you back where you live. Take you right home.

[GRAVES *shakes head – no.*]

So.

GRAVES: I can't.

CHARLIE: O.K. [*Collecting the eating instruments.*] O.K. I've got to go and do my job. I've got to clear this table then. I'm going to even have to take the table cloth, even the chairs, even the table. So no use waiting. That kind of guy just never comes back. What do you want to waste time waiting for. Come on. You going to go out with me?

[GRAVES *shakes head – no.*]

O.K. sister, it's your life. I tell you, you're wasting your time waiting. [CHARLIE *turning with his tray full to take them away, stops, comes back.*] Look, kid, say let me get you an apple. I don't want to see you just sitting here.

GRAVES: I'm all right.

CHARLIE: Have an apple. Free.

[GRAVES *shakes head – no.*]

Have [*reaching to breast pocket*] a piece of chewing gum.

[GRAVES *shakes head – no.*]

[CHARLIE *turns to kitchen with tray full,* FRITZ *comes out. Charlie to Fritz.*] She won't budge, see what you done.

FRITZ: The table's got to be cleared that's all.

CHARLIE [*muttering*]: Yeah, that's all, that's all.

FRITZ [*at Graves's table*]: Look, Miss, I've got my orders and I got to keep my job. Don't listen to this waiter. All he's looking for is some innocent kid who don't know what she's doing to go out with him. He's three kids. I counted them myself. And his wife's so fat she can't walk. Can't even get near enough to kiss her. Just what he deserves. You see, you can't trust anybody. [*Lifting tablecloth from table.*] Like I'm saying I've got to do my job.

[CHARLOTTE *taking her elbows from table as cloth comes up.* FRITZ *folding it.*]

Just like the waiter, give you a rose that don't belong to him. [FRITZ *takes cloth to pantry, passing Charlie.*] Baby snatcher.

CHARLIE: What's a matter, jealous?

FRITZ [*into pantry*]: Some Romeo.

CHARLIE [*comes, puts his hands on Christian's chair*]: I've got to take this, honey, you're making this the saddest day of my life. [CHARLIE *shaking head.*] I feel it.

[*Faintly the Humming Chorus from Madame Butterfly.* CHARLIE *takes chair away.* FRITZ *comes out. Lurks.* CHARLIE *comes out. They take each one a pot of the white waving grass away.*

Lights fade. And take the flowers from the walls. They come back and FRITZ *gives Charlie a nod of command. Both to the table, one on each side,* CHARLOTTE *lifts her elbows, puts clenched fists against her cheeks, and they carry the table away.* GRAVES *sits on the edge of her chair.* CHARLIE *and* FRITZ *come hesitant towards her.* FRITZ *nods to Charlie.* CHARLIE *hesitates. Then both take chair.*]

FRITZ [*hands on chair*]: Sorry, Miss, but we can't help it. we've got to take your chair.

CHARLIE: Sorry kid.

[CHARLOTTE GRAVES *slides forward. They step back.* CHARLOTTE *to her knees in front of empty chair.* FRITZ *and* CHARLIE *each hesitating to take it and both go to take it and lift it away.* CHARLOTTE GRAVES *alone, her*

*clenched fists up over her eyes as she kneels and silently
weeps. Outside an afternoon turned to night.* FRITZ *and*
CHARLIE *pausing at pantry door, chair held between
them, and look back over their shoulders at Charlotte
Graves, and then at each other.*]

You lousy rat.

FRITZ: You lousy rat.

[FRITZ *and* CHARLIE *enter pantry.*

*Momentarily at the high factory window, the head and
shoulders of* CORNELIUS CHRISTIAN *as he kneels,
looking in on this sadness, the trembling lonely figure of
Charlotte Graves. The latter part of the Humming Chorus.*

CHRISTIAN *enters this restaurant. Standing, an Admiral
on his bridge at the top of the stairs, in grey topper, tails
and white tie, evening cane tucked under his arm, as he
waits in the sudden bright rising lights and the fading end
of the Humming Chorus. Bare feet resplendent, a large
sparkling diamond on each toe.*]

CHARLIE [*appearing at pantry door. A gander at this scene*]:
Holy mackerel.

FRITZ [*appearing behind Charlie*]: What's this, somebody
arrived? A personage.

CHARLIE: I should live so long.

FRITZ: Shut up, maybe you won't. Get out the table.
[FRITZ *forward to receive this glistening guest. To take his
hat and cane. And with an open arm welcome him to proceed.*]
Sir.

CHRISTIAN: Thank you.

[CHRISTIAN *pausing to give a general perusement of feet
and the large sparkling diamonds, goes with the slow step,
wearing the frozen smile of the potentate across his*

appearance, and moves down into the midst of this pre-posterous eatery.

CHARLOTTE GRAVES *rises, goes forward to Christian. Lays her head on his brave chest. And they stand, waiting and watching the feverish preparation of their table by tricky Charlie and Fritz.*]

FRITZ [CHARLIE *placing the table. Rushing back and returning with cloth.* FRITZ *flattening the creases.* CHARLIE *out and back with vase of flowers, places them on table, hesitates.* FRITZ *arranging flowers, turns to Charlie using the side whisper*]: The condiments and cutlery, you fool, fast.

CHARLIE: Oh, yeah. [*Off and back with tray, the condiments, and eating instruments. The laying of instruments.* CHARLIE *picking up a plate, brief examination in light, a flash wipe of the sleeve. The wide eyes of good old Fritz.*]

FRITZ [*with large menus tucked under arm.* FRITZ *beckoning to Christian*]: Sir. Madam. [*Eyelids are fluttering every-where,* CHRISTIAN *steps high-footed forward.* CHARLIE *at action station at Christian's chair.* FRITZ *does for Madam. And this couple are gently seated. A flourish of arm and* FRITZ *makes the presentation of menus.*] Good evening, madam. Good evening, sir.

CHRISTIAN: Good evening. What's choice?

FRITZ: May I be so bold as to suggest the *consommé en gelée.*

CHRISTIAN: Ah, Charlotte? [*Shakes head – yes.*]

FRITZ [*to Charlotte*]: Might madam like some kind of fish to follow?

GRAVES: Shrimps.

FRITZ [*on his little pad*]: Crustaceans for madam.

CHRISTIAN: Smoked salmon.

FRITZ: *Saumon fumé* for sir. And to follow, sir? For Madam?

GRAVES: Steak.

FRITZ: Mignon.

GRAVES: I guess so.

FRITZ: Rare?

GRAVES: Yes.

FRITZ: Garlic?

GRAVES [*to Christian*]: Should I?

CHRISTIAN: Feel free.

GRAVES: Garlic.

FRITZ: Very good, madam. Vegetables? Madam?

GRAVES: Asparagus.

FRITZ: Sir?

CHRISTIAN: Asparagus.

FRITZ: Asparagus for two. Potatoes? Madam?

GRAVES: Boiled.

FRITZ: For sir?

CHRISTIAN: Fried.

[CHRISTIAN *with his silver cigarette case, which looks like platinum for this occasion. Offering Charlotte a cigarette. She takes it. An awkward putting in the mouth.*]

FRITZ [*diving to assist. The striking of a match*]: Allow me madam.

[*The sunset smile as Madam blows out that first puff. And he then retreats, using the backward lifting step, head inclined for and towards Christian, this present potentate.*]

CHARLIE [*with pitcher of water, pincers, and lemon peel*]: Good evening, sir.

CHRISTIAN: Good evening.

CHARLIE: Good evening, madam.

GRAVES: Hello.

CHARLIE [*pouring and poised with pincers*]: Will madam have some peel? [*Nod of yes.*] And for sir?

CHRISTIAN: Ah. I think so.

CHARLIE [*a bow*]: I hope the water will be to your satisfaction. [*The backward retreat.*]

FRITZ [*waiting with high sniffing sneer as* CHARLIE *backs by him, and* FRITZ *holds a satin stool aloof in his hands.* CHARLIE *looking at stool, backs into wall.* FRITZ *with dignity proceeds to table. To* CHRISTIAN] Sir. May I? For your feet, sir.

CHRISTIAN: Ah.

FRITZ [*placing it.* CHRISTIAN *crosses tootsies on velvet stool*]: Make sir more comfortable.

CHRISTIAN: Ah. Thank you.

FRITZ: A pleasure, sir. And now perhaps, sir, would like something to drink. [*Another menu handed over.*] A white wine to start with, perhaps. With the *poisson* and madam's crustaceans. [*A pointing finger.*] I can recommend this one.

CHRISTIAN: Cordial.

FRITZ: Very good, sir. [*Retreating with the backward step and genuflected head.*]

GRAVES [*a hand forward over Christian's hand*]: I'm sorry.

CHRISTIAN [*Christian, that forgiver of all minor sins*]: That's all right. You see [*Christian presenting a foot*], the colour of this, too, is peach.

CURTAIN

APPLAUSE